CHRISTIANITY AND THE WEST

The John Henry Cardinal Newman Lectures

GENERAL EDITOR: *Craig Steven Titus*

The John Henry Cardinal Newman Lecture Series is held under the sponsorship of the Institute for the Psychological Sciences in order to promote an international conversation among the several disciplines that treat the human person. This Washington-based lecture series is held annually, and forthcoming volumes will be published with an eye toward building a body of learned discussion that is catholic both in its breadth of research and in its dialogue with contemporary Catholic thought. The published versions appear under the patronage of St. Catherine of Alexandria in order to demonstrate the conviction of those responsible for the Newman lecture series that the human person flourishes only when the Creator of heaven and earth is loved above all things.

The John Henry Cardinal Newman Lectures

VOLUME 3

CHRISTIANITY AND THE WEST

Interaction and Impact in Art and Culture

EDITED BY *Craig Steven Titus*

The Institute for the Psychological Sciences Press
Arlington, Virginia

Distributed by
The Catholic University of America Press
620 Michigan Ave., N.E. / 240 Leahy Hall
Washington, DC 20064

The paper used in this publication meets the minimum requirements of
American National Standards for Information Science—Permanence of Paper
for Printed Library Materials, ANSI Z39.48-1984.
∞

LIBRARY OF CONGRESS CATALOGING-IN-PUBLICATION DATA
Christianity and the West : interaction and impact in art and culture / edited
by Craig Steven Titus.
        p. cm. — (The John Henry Cardinal Newman lectures ; V. 3)
        Includes bibliographical references and index.
        ISBN 978-0-9773103-2-6 (pbk. : alk. paper)   1. Christianity and culture.
2. Christianity and the arts.   I. Titus, Craig Steven, 1959–
        BR115.C8C4467 2009   2008040515
        306.6′3091821—dc22

CONTENTS

ACKNOWLEDGMENTS

In the name of the Institute for Psychological Sciences, I would like to acknowledge the many actors who contributed to making possible this collection of essays from the 2003–2004 John Henry Cardinal Newman Lecture Series. First of all, I would like to recognize the faithful generosity of Gene and Charlotte Zurlo, who have funded the Newman Lecture Series from its inception. Furthermore, because of Dr. John Harvey's benevolent sponsorship, the lectures were held at the Cosmos Club (Washington, D.C.), which has continued to offer a fitting ambiance for genteel discussions. The corporate and personal authorities of the Institute for the Psychological Sciences (Arlington, Va.) have warmly encouraged the publication of these lectures. Dr. David McGonagle, director of the Catholic University of America Press, and his staff have contributed their competent and careful aid in bringing this volume to fruition, as have Susan Barnes (copyeditor) and Roman Lokhmotov, Cristina Melendez, Anthony Bond, and Gregory Bottaro (graduate assistants). Finally, I would like to acknowledge the foresight of Prof. Daniel N. Robinson, who inspired this series, and the commitment and energy of Dean Gladys Sweeney, who mobilized a host of prominent scholars and organized the series and this publication.

CHRISTIANITY AND THE WEST

Craig Steven Titus

INTRODUCTION

Western culture and art were not born of unknown parents. Christianity, while receiving its mother tongues and its first canonical texts within the Hebrew and Greco-Roman civilizations, has provided its own major contributions to the art and culture of the last two millennia. In this volume, scholars of international reputation, clerics and lay, Protestant and Catholic, have reflected on how Christ transforms all manner of human endeavor and on how, throughout this era, Christians have dialogued with surrounding cultures and religions, even as they blazed pathways unique to the Gospel. The contributors scrutinize past achievements in order to glean insights that serve to face the postmodern secularization of Western society and the globalization of communication, trade, and travel that seem to claim a right to creative experimentation that is free from longstanding values and detached from communities where the quality of culture and art makes a difference.[1] The contributors practice one or more of the following: playwright, film critic, architect, novelist, philosopher, theologian. In order to assist the reader in understanding their work,

---

1. This situation is outlined in *La culture à l'épreuve de la mondialisation*, ed. Jacques Poulain (Paris: UNESCO, 2004).

I would like to delimit the concepts of culture and art afoot in this volume, before doing the same for Christianity and for the West.

The etymology of the word "culture" is found in the Latin verb *colere* and its past participle *cultus*. The former initially meant to cultivate with care crops and animals, especially to till the soil; afterwards, it was applied to the cultivation of human beings that has produced the cumulative achievements of societies and the notable works of individuals. "*Cultus*," for its part, refers particularly to divine worship. Christianity has recognized a correlation between the three uses of "culture" concerning nature, humanity, and God; human culture and even agriculture are incomplete if they are not identified as gifts that elicit a response of *cultus* or the praise and thanks found in religion.

Cicero uses "*cultura*" in reference to the cultivation of human nature: "As fertile as a field may be, it cannot be productive without culture, and it is the same for humans without teaching." He notes that philosophy's role is to establish "culture of the soul."[2] Cicero's insight, which represents Greco-Roman educative tradition of *paideia*, has been carried over in the Western understanding of how an educative project above all imparts culture, thereby making people capable of appreciating cultural achievements and of contributing their own. Jacques Maritain, in his *Religion et culture*,[3] also transfers the image of cultivation from fields to the human domain. A field left unattended does yield growth, but of wild things; its cultivation provokes what is otherwise not possible. Intelligent efforts, similarly, provoke a growth of human culture that is otherwise impossible. Maritain founds genuine culture in human nature, the potential of which can be expressed either in wild ways or in ways of excellence; examples of the latter are found in the creative work produced not by dumb luck, but by the

---

2. Marcus Tullius Cicero, *Tusculan Disputations*, trans. E. J. King (Cambridge: Harvard University Press, 1973) II.5.13. In the English language, the first figurative use of "culture" for human education is attested in 1510 (*Oxford English Dictionary*, 1983).

3. Jacques Maritain, *Religion and Culture*, trans. J. F. Scanlan (London: Sheed and Ward, 1931). See also his *True Humanism*, trans. M. R. Adamson (London: Geoffrey Bles: The Centenary Press, 1941).

acquired skills called virtues, including the intellectual virtues of wisdom *(sapientia)*, knowledge *(scientia)*, and art *(ars)*.

The term "art" is widely used to signify the aesthetic principles, theoretical knowledge, and practical techniques used to create works of artistic value.[4] Jacques Maritain defines the word "art" as a creative activity of the human spirit, as a human capacity and practical virtue concerned directly with the fruitful accomplishment of a work (the *bonum operis*).[5] Moreover, he holds that art, like poetry, is first of all a communication between the interior being of things and the interior being of man. After extensive reflection on art, poetry, and creativity, Maritain came to hold that the artist's knowledge of truth (a poetic knowledge that is presupposed by arts of all kinds) is a connatural knowledge, a type of pre-conceptual cognition of a creative or exemplar idea through union with the beloved person or thing.[6] This love for the object of art makes the artist a contemplative, who rejoices in her cognitive and affective union. The artist, though, unlike the pure theoretician or contemplative, also seeks practical expression of the creative intuitions born of this contemplation. The artist seeks to develop a practical virtue that makes her good at judging how to convey beauty,[7] She does so in created things, but also in herself. The scholastics thus spoke of *natura* and second nature *(habitus)* in interconnected ways

4. For an overview of modern conception of art and aesthetics, see Roger Scruton, *An Intelligent Person's Guide to Modern Culture* (South Bend, IN: St. Augustine's Press, 2000), especially pages 30–46.

5. Jacques Maritain's major contributions to a theory of art are found in his *Creative Intuition in Art and Poetry* (New York: Pantheon Books, 1953) and *Art and Scholasticism with Other Essays*, trans. J. F. Scanlan (Whitefish, MT: Kessinger Publishing, 2003).

6. See Maritain, *Creative Intuition*, chap. VII; Aquinas, *De Veritate (Disputed Questions on Truth)* qq. 3 and 4; Ralph McInerny, *Art and Prudence: Studies in the Thought of Jacques Maritain* (Notre Dame, IN: University of Notre Dame Press, 1988), pp. 153 and 172.

7. For Aquinas, art attains beauty when it is expressing integrity or wholeness *(integritas or perfectio)*, proportion or harmony *(proportio or consonantia)*, and clarity or radiance *(claritas)*. Moreover, beauty has a likeness to the Son of God on these three counts. See *Summa theologiae* I q. 39, a. 8.

(based on the normativeness of nature) rather than in constructivist ways (where variation knows no native boundaries). The union "culture and art," as found in the creative human being, refers to intellectual and practical dispositions that make up science and art, as well as the dispositions that make up the moral and the theological culture expressed in the other virtues.

Josef Pieper, for his part, recognizes that the quality of true culture and art is assured by a notion of leisure and worship that puts human efforts into the larger context of human fulfillment; the notion of fulfillment includes the human need for feasts, festivals, and faith.[8] Divinely established festivals and periods of rest from labor allow people to focus on what is ultimate (God) and thereby to be revived from toil; such is the case because rest, contemplation, and worship are expressive of a receptive bearing. Pieper argues that this receptivity is the basis for true cultural and artistic achievements.[9] It is found in Plato, Aristotle,[10] the Judeo-Christian Scriptures, and philosophy. Aquinas, too, gives receptivity a primordial role in human action by correlating two aspects of knowledge, namely, intellectual vision *(intellectus)* and discursive reason *(ratio)*. The former includes the essential insight *(simplex intuitus)* or basic understanding of the beauty of the world, oneself, and God; it provides principles and context for the discursive work of searching, abstracting, refining, and judging.[11]

The role of a receptive gaze or intellectual vision is denied in notions, such as in certain readings of Kant's *Critic of Pure Reason,* that give undue weight to the "discursive" effort in the act of knowledge.[12]

---

8. Josef Pieper, *Leisure: The Basis of Culture,* trans. Gerald Malsbary (South Bend, IN: St. Augustine's Press, 1998).

9. Ibid., pp. 4–26.

10. Aristotle grants leisure a pivotal role in the life of the person and city. He says: "the first principle of all action is leisure" (*Politics* bk. VII, ch. 3, 1337b33); that happiness depends on it (*Nicomachean Ethics* bk. X, ch. 7, 1177b4–6); and that speculative sciences were born of it (*Metaphysics* bk. I, ch. 1, 981b20–22).

11. See Aquinas, *De Veritate* q. 15, a. 1; and Pieper, *Leisure,* p. 11.

12. See Josef Pieper's comments on Immanuel Kant's *Critic of Pure Reason* (Lei-

Acceptance of Kant's focus on the human subject has lead modern thinkers to emphasize the intellectual work of the philosopher and also useful work, to the detriment of the roles of nature and God as archetypical sources for human culture and art. Pieper recognized that the "work for work's sake" mentality, which he found in post–World War II Marxism and in National Socialism, instrumentalizes the person for the ends of production and makes the claim that labor is the entirety of life.[13] Similar stances are found in liberal democracies: in attempts to maximize performance at work, success in sports, and creativity in artistic ventures, even with risky or illegal pharmacological supports; and in the "entertainment for entertainment's sake" and "art for art's sake" mentalities, which motivate people without any ultimate goal. When cut off from ultimate notions, such as festival and faith, valuing only useful work or aesthetic pleasure can lead to totalitarianism, relativism, or the deconstruction of culture and the person. One particularly disturbing strain of thought, which is led by a hermeneutic of suspicion, terminates in a single value to promote: bodies and pleasures, as Michel Foucault and, more recently, Judith Butler would have us believe.[14]

Culture and art rest on theoretical, intuitive, and referential foundations. For Pieper, the basis of culture is the true leisure (*otium* in Latin, *Musse* in German) that is not simply the absence of work, but the presence of purpose, meaning, and ultimate ends. Leisure is based

---

sure, pp. 9–17). Kant's treatment of art and taste is found in his critique of aesthetic judgment.

13. See Bernard Schumacher's "Preface" to the French translation of Josef Pieper's book on leisure: *Le Loisir, fondement de la culture* (Geneva: Ad solem, 2007); and Frank Töpfer, "Josef Pieper and the Spiritual Foundations of Totalitarianism," in *A Cosmopolitan Hermit: Modernity and Tradition in the Philosophy of Josef Pieper,* ed. B. Schumacher (Washington D.C.: The Catholic University of America Press, forthcoming [2009]).

14. Michel Foucault, *The History of Sexuality,* vol. I: *An Introduction,* trans. Robert Hurley (New York: Random House, 1978); Judith Butler, *Subjects of Desire: Hegelian Reflections in Twentieth-Century France* (New York: Columbia University Press, 1999). On this point, I am indebted to David Franks's research.

upon sacrifice and sacrament: the former values gift, and the latter mediates the invisible through the visible. The result is a condition of the soul—inner focus, stillness, and absence of preoccupation—fed by the gift of insight and contemplation.[15] With this vision of leisure as the necessary condition for contemplation, the stage has been set for us to begin to understand the relationship between useful arts *(artes serviles)* and liberal ones *(artes liberales)*.[16] The useful arts, on the one hand—art, craft, trade, or profession—are indispensable for human survival; the liberal arts , on the other, in various ways approach the underlying gratuitousness of being that is appreciated in contemplation and in festivals. The reflective posture of these latter two is available to all as a condition of the soul, but to only a few as a way of life.

True art, culture, and philosophical knowledge flow from a sense of wonder[17] and are valued as the result of the contemplation of reality, the love of existence, and the search for ultimateness. This construal of art and its foundations responds to the debate about art's social role and the artist's ethical responsibility. It defends both autonomy of artistic expression and responsibility of the artist. The greatness of the artist as artist does not make its possessor morally good or socially accountable. Beyond his artistic talent and the virtue of art, the artist must call on other strengths of character in order to adjudicate responsibility for his art, for himself, and for the common good; it is the moral virtues that perfect the agent and enable the good use of art.[18] Therefore, even if the value of the work cannot be reduced to the

15. Pieper, *Leisure*, p. 30.

16. Aristotle, *Metaphysics* bk. I, ch. 2, 982b27; Aquinas, *Commentary on the Metaphysics of Aristotle* bk. I, n. 59 and *Summa theologiae* I-II q. 57, a. 3, ad 3; Newman, *The Idea of a University* (New Haven: Yale University Press, 1966), Discourses 5 and 6; Pieper, *Leisure*, pp. 21–26, 37–38.

17. Pieper (*Leisure*, p. 62) concurs with Aquinas's observation: "The reason that the philosopher can be compared to the poet is that both are concerned with wonder *[miranda]*" (*Commentary on the Metaphysics of Aristotle* bk. I, n. 55).

18. *Summa theologiae* Ia-IIae q. 57, a. 3, ad 2; IIa-IIae q. 47, a. 8. See also Ralph McInerny, *Art and Prudence*, p. 150.

moral quality of its maker or to the service it renders to others,[19] art, like philosophy, serves the contemplative end that is fitting of humanity; both lead from encounters of wonder to encounters of meaning and belonging. Against materialist justifications for work, moreover, a realist conception of leisure, contemplation, and worship provides not only the basis for culture but also the understanding that humanizes labor and leads to a notion of justice that is transcendent at its apex and human in its expanse.[20]

The other two elements in this volume's title are "Christianity" and "the West." The term "the West" circumscribes the liberal-democratic nation-state experience found in European and American societies. However, the effects of international politics and funding, multinational corporations, and the communication of ideas have extended "the West." A focus on the West does not deny Christianity's influence elsewhere or pigeonhole it as a regional phenomenon; rather, that focus identifies the influence that the Church of Christ and the message of the Gospel have had in Western art and culture. Christianity's role has changed over time and in the various parts of Western civilization, from first-century persecutions, though periods of accommodation and revolt, into the modern and postmodern West, where a type of tolerance has pushed some Christians to confine expression of their convictions to the private realm. Modern history traces different Western experiments with the separation of church and state. The way this separation is played out in politics and law has set the stage for Christianity's influence on culture and art.[21]

19. Jacques Maritain, *The Responsibility of the Artist* (New York: Gordian Press, 1972). See also Etienne Gilson, *The Arts of the Beautiful* (Champaign, IL: Dalkey Archives Press, 2000).

20. From Leo XIII to Benedict XVI, Catholic social teaching has addressed the question of work and justice in the context of humanity's ultimate origin and vocation. See especially Leo XIII, On Capital and Labor, *Rerum Novarum* (May 15, 1891); John Paul II, On Human Work, *Laborem Exercens* (September 14, 1981); and Benedict XVI, On God's Love, *Deus caritas est* (December 25, 2005).

21. For complementary understandings of this impact, see Stanley Hauerwas's

In the face of diverse Western trains of thought, Christianity—through its faithful, its leaders, its teachings, and its cultural and artistic achievements—has provided a living memory for humanity, above all for humankind's spiritual nature and aspirations. That the physical and spiritual dimensions of person and of culture form a unity is an oft-forgotten truth. "The word 'culture' in its general sense indicates everything whereby man develops and perfects his many bodily and spiritual qualities," *Gaudium et spes* tells us.[22] In this view, culture is human nature played out in time through knowledge and effort.

In the academic study of culture, it should be noted, the social sciences have explored culture in terms of values and ideas, practices and customs, laws and rules, institutions and artifacts.[23] However, social science accounts neither fully respond to humankind's deepest questions nor clearly adjudicate between values, thereby tending to relativize human aspirations and efforts.[24] From a Catholic perspec-

---

essay in this volume and Michael Novak, "The First Institution of Democracy: Tocqueville on Religion," in *The Person and the Polis: Faith and Values within the Secular State*, ed. C. S. Titus (Washington, D.C.: The IPS Press, 2006), pp. 132–52.

22. The Second Vatican Council, *The Church in the Modern World, Gaudium et Spes* (December 7, 1965), n. 53.

23. UNESCO, moreover, has given a composite sociological definition of culture as "the whole complex of distinctive spiritual, material, intellectual and emotional features that characterize a society or social group. It includes not only the arts and letters, but also modes of life, the fundamental rights of the human being, value systems, traditions and beliefs" ("Mexico City Declaration on Cultural Policies," World Conference on Cultural Policies, Mexico City, 26 July–6 August 1982). A thematic approach would continue by distinguishing high from popular culture; culture from civilization; the cultural product of a group or an individual; culture from commercialized media; nature from culture; culture from subcultures; and so on.

24. This relativization of values has caused the unprecedented crisis of incommensurability in cultural anthropology and its neighboring disciplines. Alasdair MacIntyre traces such epistemological crises in the sciences, in his *The Task of Philosophy: Selected Essays*, vol. 1 (Cambridge: Cambridge University Press, 2006). Unfortunately, religion in general as well as and Christianity in particular is often construed as a spare appendix, either made obsolete by science or lacking an integral connection with the whole person or society. Nonetheless, this tendency is corrected in some studies of the sociology of religion.

tive, respect for the methodological competencies of the social sciences does not justify the denial of either human spiritual nature and values or the influence that Christianity has had on the West's foundations and institutions, practices of care and of hospitality, and so forth.

Needless to say, one cannot identify Christianity and the West, not only because of other influences, but also because Christianity is an affair of the Gospel, which transcends cultures, while at the same time being transported by them. While admitting the need for translation, the Gospel (which means Good News and renders the Greek *euangelion*) is more an event than a text; it is also an initiative of God rather than of human beings. In his encyclical on charity, Pope Benedict XVI states that "being Christian is not the result of an ethical choice or a lofty idea, but the encounter with an event, a person, which gives life a new horizon and a decisive direction."[25] In this assertion of the centrality of faith, Benedict is not denying the import of ethics or theology in the life of the Christian; rather he is affirming that faith is both a gift from God and a personal engagement. Moreover, the Gospel is not exhausted when it inspires a particular instance of culture or art, which represents the Kingdom of God. God's Kingdom is central even if we cannot yet fully fathom it or ever empirically measure it. A sympathetic reading of Christianity's place in the West will at least admit that Christianity is a monotheistic faith, confident in the presence of God, centered on his Son and his Church, whose life of grace (of the Holy Spirit) is communicated to people through the words and gestures that make up the divinely revealed Scriptures and the divinely instituted sacraments of faith. This context sheds light on the correlative needs for an evangelization of each culture and for a cultural understanding of the Gospel.

The Christian perspective resists one-dimensional categorizations that sometimes emerge from the social sciences or philosophy. It seeks, rather, multidimensional philosophical principles and reflections to

25. *Deus caritas est* (December 25, 2005), n. 1.

help understand the interplay of religion, art, and culture. At the heart of this vision, culture and art, as a body of knowledge and achievements that animate people and communities, provides the practices that humanize experience and that constitute the means for achieving human potential. The particularly Catholic perspective on culture manifests itself (1) by a humble optimism about the perfectibility of human beings and communities (that have a potential trajectory of development) in God's plan and in the ambit of his gratuitous grace; and (2) by the place of Christ and his Church in culture. Benedict XVI made this last point clear when affirming that the challenges of secularization and sects are best faced when efforts are completely centered on Christ and his Church's mediations of God's presence, especially as his presence is found in the sacraments of his Church.[26] This program for action must be understood in the context of the Church's belief in the role of reason in a dialogue of cultures and religions, as affirmed in Benedict XVI's much discussed Regensburg address, "On Faith, Reason and the University."[27] Culture risks becoming destructive when the aesthetic is severed from sources of faith and reason about human origins and ends. In order to face this risk, the present volume seeks to explore the impact that Christianity has had in art and culture in the West, especially in the fields of fine art and architecture, literature and social criticism, theater, cinema, and politics.

In his article, John Haldane examines the roles that nature and art play in providing the human quest with intimations of a transcendent and creative cause, whom we call God. Granting nature a status independent of human constructs yet accessible to human knowledge makes no small difference in its role as a vehicle for human meaning and aesthetic appreciation. Nature manifests design not only for

26. See his Address, Inaugural Session of the Fifth General Conference of the Bishops of Latin America and the Caribbean, May 13, 2007.

27. Pope Benedict XVI, Lecture at the University of Regensburg (September 12, 2006).

St. Paul (Rom 1:20), but also for Stoic thinkers, who find that the invisible attributes of divine power are made known by the beauty and order of earth, sun, moon, and stars. For poets like Gerard Manley Hopkins, nature, although "seared with trade; bleared, smeared with toil" is never spent and moreover continues to evidence not only external signs of past creative activity, but also signs of ongoing expressions of divinity. Nonetheless, both specialized and popular debates have made it clear that much is at stake in the different visions of naturalism, creationism, and design. On the side that avows nature as the product of creative design, one seeks to avoid identifying God with nature or making God a part of nature (pantheism and panentheism) while affirming the active presence of God as cause of the existence and natures of things even as they develop. Haldane explores two types of argument that affirm design: arguments from natural order and those from the experience of beauty in nature. Arguments from design and aesthetic sensibility must face a host of objections. Is nature really beautiful? Or is it only apparently so due to human projections or our selection of what pleases and suits our purposes? Is beauty in nature a mere product of chance or does it have an evolutionary explanation? Haldane defends design arguments from naturalist, materialist, reductionist, and evolutionary detractors. He affirms a classical starting point, that "there is beauty in nature," which provides the basis for reasoning that this beauty, as with other artwork, should be attributed to a divine creator-designer. Although this classical perspective will displease agnostic and atheistic thinkers and delight some religious thinkers, another strain of religious thought (Plato and Petrarch) struggles against the sensory world, which it construes as a distraction from what is the foremost priority, namely, the spiritual life. This view contains dualist features that need to be addressed in order to resolve the problem of how to correlate sense pleasure and attractiveness with spiritual joy and splendor. An Idealist dualism pits the sensual experience of beauty and the body against the thought of moral, intellectual, and spiritual life: we can be concerned about either nature and the senses or the soul and ultimate causes, but not both. However, such confusions are resolved when these primordial oppositions are overcome. Attempts to clarify these images and rise above these dualities have been made by art, philosophy, and religion. In the case of art, the issue is to use both material and craft in expressing beauty and ideas. But what affinity should nature have to art and art to nature? On this last point, arts of different sorts aid in reconnecting an often alienated public with a hunger to rediscover the beauty of nature and to recognize that it is embodied with God's greatness.

Culture and art are also expressed through the buildings, monuments, and churches that constitute our cities and towns. Carroll William Westfall addresses how architecture in the West has been impacted by Christianity's authority and its need for a representational art capable both of signifying a deeper meaning and of symbolizing what is otherwise invisible. In particular, Westfall appraises four contributions that Christianity has made in its long-standing alliance with the art of architecture. First, Christian architecture made it normative to have an axial arrangement of interrelated interior spaces (narthex, nave, sanctuary) that are significant in themselves and that take their meaning from the activities held therein. This Constantinian innovation made the liturgy accessible to all initiated believers by integrating Egyptian, Greco-Roman, and Hebraic elements. Second, Christianity invested its ecclesial architecture with a content-rich beauty that communicates the position of beauty in a moral universe. Through a merging of theology, aesthetics, and architectural theory, St. Augustine, Dionysius, the Scholastics, and Renaissance thinkers expressed in various ways that such beauty symbolizes God's love and the order He has established in the universe. Third, the role of architecture (and of the architect) in society became recognized as influencing the moral well-being of its citizens. Starting with the theoretical and practical contributions of Filippo Brunelleschi (1377–1446), the architect was understood to have the role of building the city of man in order to serve the City of God. Finally, in the Christian West, the architect's role became that of imitating God's work of creation. Thus, Leon Battista Alberti (1404–1472) drew together Vitruvius's classical theory of architecture (with its criteria of *symmetria, eurythmia,* and *decor*), the Scholastic notion of beauty, and Brunelleschi's invention of perspective in the service of understanding and expressing enduring principles that God uses to create nature. Subsequent developments in the practice and theory of architecture have furtively challenged or openly refuted certain of these contributions to Western culture. In particular, the Reformation, the Enlightenment, and Modernism have tended to erode, or at least displace, the link between architecture and its role of signifying and symbolizing an authoritative and doctrinal content to its work. Moreover, Westfall argues that the disestablishment of religious institutions and the secularization of governmental authority have promoted an inverse relationship between justice and the quality of cities. Individualized notions of rights and polity have eclipsed communitarian ends and the latter's expression in public architecture. Architecture has often become construed as independent of any authority that might call it to the service of institutions—secular or sacred—that serve the common good. In conclusion, Westfall draws a parallel between this situation and that of modern philosophy. He intimates that Pope John Paul II's encyclical *Fides et Ratio* provides a model to promote a renewed role for architecture in serving faith. Within a variety of architectural forms that serve religion, we should expect that reason and the architectural trade can collaborate in the task of constructing buildings that embody the goodness, truth, and beauty that reside at the heart of the Church and of Western culture and polity.

Literature is a privileged agent in the integration of Christianity and culture, as Ralph McInerny knows in theory and in practice. He makes the case that treating Catholic things does not of itself make for great literature. The capacity of all literature to speak some transcendent truth—which Flannery O'Connor perceives as the anagogical nature of literature—does not eliminate the need to rank literature against a standard. While some good books deserve to be read but once, a practical criterion would be, according to C. S. Lewis, whether we are drawn to reread the work. The determinative criterion, though, is the profundity of the author's insight into the mystery of human action as conveyed in the imaginative interweaving of setting, plot, character, language, and humor. The Catholic difference attends to not only the natural gratification, success, or flourishing, but the issue of what is truly fulfilling, that is, what offers some participation in supernatural beatitude, as Aquinas would have us understand. Differentiating Catholic authors, for McInerny, comes down to deciphering how they put their characters in the light of ultimate salvation and damnation. The rank increases as the supernatural stakes of action are played out more intensely, cease to be side issues and become the story. Such is the interest of Dante and Bernanos, who, McInerny asserts, have a unique status in this regard. They cast their characters in the light of ultimate evil or good. Bernanos, for his part, subtly nuances his characters to illustrate the essential differences between moral failure and evil and between heroism and sanctity. In novels such as *Diary of a Country Priest* (1936), the subject of fiction, the responsible agent with an ultimate purpose, provides a corrective to modern fiction that is contented with triviality. Bernanos resisted the tendency to mechanize human life, to let power have the last word, or to let numbers dominate the world (*France against the Robots*, 1944). His pastoral perception of every character exposes their present goals to an ultimate assessment of the mystery of the human person. Bernanos thus demonstrates how Christian literature can cast the human person in the light of his ultimate destiny, which provides a counterbalance to banality and also a direction for the journey.

Theater is a unique means of expressing culture and influencing it. While the script bears the plot, the intention of the author, and indications for the scene, it is the director's interpretation of a play, its performance, and the contact between actor and audience that distinguish it from literature or the cinema. Peter John Cameron addresses theater's specificity and the role that it plays in evangelizing culture. As Luigi Giussani observes, the theater's advantage is its capacity to gain access to the personal level, where the Christian drama is played out. For John Paul II, the basic human tragedy is to fail to perceive the meaning of one's life, for wont of something that inspires one to search for the truth of the human "I." The theater's vocation is just that, to incite the human search for meaning. According to Hans Urs von Balthasar, the theater's task is to make the human drama explicit and to nurture the habit of looking further, higher, and deeper than the obvious: human existence is theater and the "I" is its role. Aristotle taught that human beings were compelled to observe dramatic imitations of human action in order to discover something of their own destiny. The playwright and novelist Thornton Wilder believed that the best strategy to provoke this search was to represent original sin dramatically, that is, to show the vainness of identifying the totality of meaning with some aspect of our self. Theater continues where discussions fall short, and creates an event that "opens us to the totality of reality" (Luigi Giussani), that expresses "objectively certain secret truths" (Antonin Arbaud), and that pushes language to its limit in search of mystery. The theater's unique interactive claim, over that of the written word, is to offer an encounter with the actor and a sense of belonging to the audience. Both Christian theology and contemporary drama theory have come to understand theater's potential to motivate through the noble aspirations and good life of the common man. As Arthur Miller said, every person can become a tragic hero, when moved by a "total compulsion to evaluate himself justly" and when drawn to anticipate and prepare to lay down his life, when need be.[28] A drama can inspire the audience to do likewise. John Paul II realized, from his own experience of the stage and the Gospel, that God became a human actor so as to offer an encounter with the One who is the source of being and action.

28. Arthur Miller, "Tragedy and the Common Man," in *The Theater Essays of Arthur Miller*, ed. Robert A. Martin and Steven R. Centola (New York: Da Capo Press, 1996), p. 5.

This mystery of God's presence and of human destiny is not destroyed by language or by drama; rather, they provide the evocative basis for faith to transform culture. As Cameron avers, theater can aid evangelization through its capacity to stimulate reason's quest for meaning, to offer an encounter with a presence, and to play to the promises contained in our deepest longings.

Does the cinema dilute the meaning of life, impersonalize drama, and impose cultural stereotypes? Or can it communicate a spiritual message and be an instrument of grace? Guy Bedouelle treats the complexity and completeness of the event, industry, and art that constitute contemporary cinema. The resources and aspirations of the cinema are great; so are the shortfalls of particular films. The resources at the cinema's disposition constitute an evocative marriage of image and sound. What cinema may lack in explicit argument, it supplements with suggestive dialogue and reflections, gestures and faces, music and silence. The cinema is not limited to the spoken word. Its capacity to communicate nonverbally is coupled with special effects that create complex impressions of time and space and suggest the intimate experiences of remembering and imagining, sensing and being moved, judgments and choosing, as well as coming to insight and belief. Cinema, however, like every practical art, cannot escape certain constraints. The dynamic of internal dialogue (even debate and torment) can be dramatized and poetically represented but hardly rendered in full, lest it overwhelm the spectator. The vision a director aspires to convey and what the spectator receives may be quite different things. This art offers experiences that are difficult to contain and impossible to control. The potential aspirations of the film makers are wide ranging. The cinema's poetic side evokes the deepest hopes and universal desires of the elite and the common man, concerning birth and death, love and history. Films do not simply seek to deliver a universal message, for they transmit a space for personal reflection, a moment of humor or entertainment; primarily, though, they seek artistic achievement. Bedouelle intimates that the cinema also has a vocation to address and nurture human spiritual yearnings. The internal dimension of the cinema speaks to the spiritual and moral overflow that comes in brushes with mystery and with the Creator. Films of Christian inspiration cast the shadow of God across the storyline through the spiritual thirst of its characters or through the contrast of disorders that exhibit a distance from the divine. Bedouelle evokes the most notable cinematographers as he explores the capacity of film to transmit grace, to offer clarity about oneself and the world, to instruct in the spiritual dimension of life and death, or to assist the viewer in discovering ultimate meaning in the midst of confusion. The capacity of the cinema to speak to the soul with poetic power derives from the incarnational nature of the cinematographic medium. Bedouelle insists that the poetic aspect of film can manifest mystery without reducing it to something less than mystery. Cinema's poetic nature, though, demands that viewers engage themselves in the reception, interpretation, and critique of the film. When viewers engage themselves, according to Bedouelle, film nourishes and revives something of the soul by creating a privileged space for personal introspection, a platform for social observation, and a renewed vision of human hope.

Today, as was the case in the wake of the American and French revolutions, debates rage concerning competing notions of culture and freedom, and in particular concerning the issue of finding liberation from certain burdens of tradition. Among the major figures that enlivened the debate in nineteenth-century Great Britain was the poet and essayist Matthew Arnold (1822–88), whose *Culture and Anarchy* (1869) analyzes culture in the face of the difficulties of the epoch. Daniel N. Robinson takes us into a philosophical exploration of culture and religion, offering a means to diagnose and treat certain difficulties past and present, by calling upon Arnold's works of political and social criticism. Arnold perceived culture as "the study of perfection," "perfection" construed as an ideal that, although ultimately unattainable, serves nonetheless to measure progress. Culture obtains knowledge of this standard by human experience (recorded in art, science, poetry, philosophy, history, and religion). Religion, like culture, seeks the ideal of perfection as an internal condition. Religion, unlike culture, comes to this conclusion directly by affirming that: "The Kingdom of God is within you." The central characteristic common to both culture and religion is that it is an internal condition, a deeply personal state of becoming something, rather than an external situation or possession. Both culture and religion are constituted by a growth of thought and feeling, wisdom and beauty, that must be weighed against the standard of dignity and happiness set by an enduring human nature. Another characteristic they share is engagement in the general welfare: the sentiment of sympathy naturally disallows any notion that separates personal welfare from the welfare of others. Cultural perfection thus is not acquired in solitude, for one cannot tend toward this perfection without carrying others along on the same path. Religion likewise secures the notion of personal happiness and development through the advancement of the Kingdom of God. These two characteristics serve to confront two major difficulties of Arnold's age: mechanism and egoism. For Arnold, ultimately the aim of culture is growth of "spirit and character" (Epictetus) and "the two noblest of things, sweetness and light" (Jonathan Swift). Against external notions of human perfection and individualism, Robinson extends Arnold's critique and guidance to the present-day challenges that face the advancement of culture and that are ultimately righted through the guidance of culture and religion. Against empty ritual, mindless habits, inauthentic friendships, addictive behavior, and other mechanical modes of thought, sentiment, and action, Robinson would have culture promote an inward perfection constituted by sweetness of disposition toward the best interests of others and by the light of knowledge of the best achievements of humankind. Robinson argues that Christianity serves an indispensable role, since the Church has bequeathed to Western civilization a score of moral, aesthetic, and civic truths and achievements, a veritable intellectual, legal, artistic, and spiritual legacy that serves not only as a guide to perfection but also as a measure of progress. In order to benefit from these truths—in a nonmechanical way—we must take them as an internal guide in the spiritual context of their whole trajectory. Thus, justice and freedom cannot be separated from an understanding of the essential nature of the human person, society, and the Church. The perfection indicated by culture and religion together point beyond our earthly senses and above our human capacity toward a transcendental good and happiness, which is best qualified as limitless in sweetness and light.

A larger treatment of culture and religion does well to address politics and Christianity, which is made poignant in the concrete. Stanley Hauerwas thus poses the question: how should the love of one's homeland, in his case America, be shaped and governed by the love of God? Or what positive impact might Christianity have on political America? Hauerwas's well-known critique of political liberalism aims to give Christians confident convictions about the intelligibility of the service they render a country. To be politically involved as Christians means, among other things, to recognize the primordial nature of the service of truthful worship of God. In opposition to liberal Protestant Christian ethics, which assumes a deep compatibility between Christianity and American democracy and between the Gospel and the American ideals of freedom and equality, Hauerwas promotes a specifically Christian contribution to the American social order. In contrast, Reinhold Niebuhr's assumption that there is no essential difference between the church and the principles of the American Experiment has rendered the dominant Protestant voice indistinct from social policy. In this context, Niebuhr and mainstream Protestants like him employ a Rawlsian construal of justice in order to formulate public policy in a diverse society. According to Nicholas Wolterstorff, however (as Hauerwas tells us), the Rawlsian notion of political unity and overlapping consensus is illusory, since no set of principles sufficient to adjudicate incommensurable conflicts is forthcoming from this liberal hypothesis. In the end, Hauerwas argues that the use of Rawls by Christians only distracts them from understanding the type of contribution

Christians might make. Another approach to the type of interaction Christians can have is found in the work of the historian of religion, Martin Marty. Borrowing from Felix Frankfurter's claim that sentiment holds society together, Marty speculates that America and its values are built upon associations that are constituted by the sentiment created through storytelling and rational argument. Alasdair MacIntyre, in contrast to Marty, takes note that such American storytelling is inherently tragic, since the habitual desire of Americans to be likeable contradicts the very base on which America is built: that is, freedom and rights undercut equality in practice and in theory. For MacIntyre, the greatest defect of the American narrative is that it seeks approval at the expense of its historical roots and in lieu of an adequate account of the future. Hauerwas emphasizes that Christians must have a first allegiance to God and to making the church the church. When Christians define "their fundamental task [to be] to make America work," they lose their ability to survive as church and they attenuate their understanding of God. For Hauerwas, a robust Christian notion of God, the crucified God, provides the hearty foundation and the content for whatever ancillary types of service Christians may render.

The creative manifestations of culture express the genius of human agents, authors, and artists, but they find their acid test in relationship with the flourishing of human persons and society. However, it is argued in this volume, a human socially astute standard is assured by the divine one. A twofold order of knowledge (the ordering of parts to a whole, and the ordering of each to the ultimate end) brings perspective to the human person in search of truth about self and the world, about ultimate origins, purpose, goals, and flourishing. This is the quest of Christians in the West who have contributed to its art and culture, as we will see in the contributions that follow.

one

John Haldane

BEAUTY, REVULSION, AND CONTEMPORARY ART

Finding God in Nature

I

Certainly there are different conceptions or understandings of the
ideas of *God,* of *nature,* and of *art,* but there have also been, and perhaps still are, altogether different concepts of these things. It strains
coherence to say that two people are merely differing in their conception of the nature of God when one allows that deity must have a material embodiment, and another denies that it may. Again, if one says
that nature is the sum total of matter in motion, and another, that it
is an integrated ecological system of flora and fauna, we should allow that they are differing over more than the right account of what is
otherwise the subject of broad definitional agreement.

Delineating the boundaries within and between concepts, and charting the course of intellectual development from one concept or conception to another requires analytical acuity and considerable historical knowledge. Here I shall not test my competence or my readers' patience by engaging extensively in these forms of conceptual and historical study: whatever the differences, it is clear enough that there is a significant tradition within Western culture (and beyond) of finding in the experience of nature, and in the making of art related to nature, intimations of a transcendent creative cause: God. For these purposes I understand *nature* to be the empirically observable material world as it is independent of human construction.[1] I take *art* to be the domain of human production in which objects (broadly construed) are created primarily for aesthetic effect, to be experienced for their compositional, expressive, and/or narrative content. And I take God to be (a) the unique ultimate cause, (b) personal, active, and providential, and (c) infinitely good, powerful, and knowledgeable.

St. Paul speaks briefly of the world as manifesting divine activity when he writes to the Romans: "Ever since the creation of the world, [God's] invisible attributes of eternal power and divinity have been able to be perceived in the things that have been made" (Romans 1:20). Far from suggesting a passing thought, however, the brevity of this remark indicates Paul's assumption that his readers were already familiar with this idea. Certainly educated people knowledgeable in the speculations of Greek and Roman philosophers and poets would have been used to the notion that nature manifests design. In words that Paul could have been echoing, a Stoic character in Cicero's *The Nature of the Gods* begins his presentation of the case for deities by saying, "What can be so obvious and clear, as we gaze up at the sky and observe the heavenly bodies, as that there is some divine power of surpassing intelligence by which they are ordered?" He later adds that the greatest reason for

---

1. Empirical observability is of course a relative notion. I have in mind the normal range of human sense-perception, in the first instance unaided but then supplemented tele- and microscopically.

believing in a creator is "the individuality, usefulness, beauty, and order of the sun and moon and stars."[2]

One might then suppose that the experience of the beauty and sublimity of nature would complement and enhance this theology of creation, and so it has for many people. Gerard Manley Hopkins made this species of aesthetic experience a central element of his poetry, sometimes lamenting that human manufacture grossly obscured the order and beauty of nature. His complaint in the latter regard goes beyond a charge of vandalism, to the charge of self-injury that impairs the power of eye to see and ear to hear the beauty of God's grandeur manifest in the natural world. He writes:

> THE WORLD is charged with the grandeur of God.
> It will flame out, like shining from shook foil;
> It gathers to a greatness, like the ooze of oil
> Crushed. Why do men then now not reck his rod?
> Generations have trod, have trod, have trod;
> And all is seared with trade; bleared, smeared with toil;
> And wears man's smudge and shares man's smell: the soil
> Is bare now, nor can foot feel, being shod.
> And for all this, nature is never spent;
> There lives the dearest freshness deep down things;
> And though the last lights off the black West went
> Oh, morning, at the brown brink eastward, springs—
> Because the Holy Ghost over the bent
> World broods with warm breast and with ah! bright wings.[3]

Evidently, like many another poet and artist before and since, Hopkins took delight in landscape and in the flora and fauna within it; he found therein not merely external evidences of creative design—in the manner of effects remaining after some activity—but

---

2. Cicero, *The Nature of the Gods,* trans. P. G. Walsh (Oxford: Claendon Press, 1997), pp. 48 and 52.

3. From "God's Grandeur," in *The Poems of Gerald Manley Hopkins,* ed. W. H. Gardner and N. H. MacKenzie (Oxford: Oxford University Press, 1970), p. 66.

ongoing expressions of divinity. It is true that one interpretation of this thought leads in the direction of *pantheism,* identifying God and nature, or *panentheism,* treating nature as part of God. But there is another way of understanding the relationship, and one licensed by orthodox Christian theology, according to which God is present in nature not spatially but actively, continuously causing the natures and existings of things. Conceived of in this way, or in ways that yield similar conclusions about the immanence of God in nature, one would welcome the experience of natural beauty as reinforcing the sense of the world as a place of creation.

Writing in the 1930s, the Cambridge philosopher and theologian F. R. Tennant, having set his face against a priori proofs of theism, interestingly developed a cumulative argument for God's existence, drawing upon a range of experienced features. He interwove the traditional argument from apparent natural order to design with an argument that proceeds from the human experience of beauty in nature to the same conclusion. He writes:

> On the telescopic and on the microscopic scale, from the starry heaven to the siliceous skeleton of the diatom [microscopic algae], in her inward parts (if scientific imagination be veridical) as well as on the surface, in flowers that "blush unseen" and gems that "unfathomed caves of ocean bear" [quoting Thomas Gray, "Elegy in a Country Churchyard"], Nature is sublime or beautiful, and the exceptions do but prove the rule. However various be the taste for beauty, and however diverse the levels of its education or degrees of its refinement, Nature elicits aesthetic sentiment from men severally and collectively.[4]

The question for Tennant is, what is it that explains the ubiquity of natural beauty? We know from our own case that, far from being invariably aesthetically pleasing, our works and products are rarely so, and then generally only when they are the products of aesthetic

---

4. F. R. Tennant, *Philosophical Theology,* vol. II: *The Soul, the World and God* (Cambridge: Cambridge University Press, 1930), p. 91.

intention, even if in association with other purposes. A mere aggregation or distribution of objects is not apt to exhibit beauty. Yet in nature, everywhere we look, we see it 'sublime or beautiful'. This degree of aesthetic value, in both extent and intensity, is inexplicable except as the intended product of design. But if there is design, then there must also be a creative "Artist" of nature whom, as Aquinas would have added, "we call God" *(et hoc dicimus Deum).*

II

Appealing as it may be, Tennant's aesthetic argument faces a series of pertinent questions. First, is it really the case that nature is generally sublime or beautiful? Second, to the extent that nature appears so to us, might not our judgments be no more than the result of our own sensibility projected onto a reality that in itself is neither beautiful nor ugly? Third, even if beauty is real, might it not be a rare phenomenon appearing ubiquitous only because we unconsciously direct our attention to what pleases us and avert our attention from and avoid what is repellent? Fourth, even if beauty is real and perhaps extensive, might it not be a product of chance? Fifth, might not our experiences of nature as appealing or significant have an evolutionary explanation?

The issue as to whether nature is really beautiful might be answered by saying that it certainly seems to be so, and that this is the recurrent testimony of human beings over time and across cultures. To this might be added the thought that, other things being equal, one should take it that things are as they generally seem to be. Combined, these two propositions yield the conclusion that, other things being equal, one should take it that nature really is beautiful. This qualified conclusion only serves, however, to direct attention to the possible ways in which other things might not be equal. Might it not be, as the second question envisages, that what we seem to find is but a reflection of our sensibility? This suggestion in turn introduces a version of the familiar question: do we find something good because it is so, or is it good because we find it to be such? Historically, philosophers were inclined to take it that our judging things to be good or bad, and beautiful or ugly, are responses to objective features. So the judgment that this or that is beautiful would be true only if the object possessed objective beauty. What this attribute might consist in remained open to debate: mathematical ratios, significant form, organic unity, are a few of the candidates; but it was generally agreed that, whatever its exact nature, beauty is a real feature of the world. Consequent upon this account is the idea that the notion of aesthetic experience is conceptually posterior to that of an aesthetic object: what makes an experience to be an aesthetic one is that it is focused on something possessed of beauty, and more precisely on the beauty of that thing.

From antiquity, however, it was always seen to be a possibility that the order of priority might run in the other direction. It might be that aesthetic objects are those things which, whatever their own character, are the objects of aesthetic experience, where the idea of such an experience is to be explained in terms of a conscious subject adopting a certain kind of attitude. By analogy, consider the claim that the view of a still pond and the sound of a small waterfall are relaxing. Are we to say that being relaxed is induced by a relaxing experience resulting from encountering a relaxing object? It is hard to believe that there are in nature such things as relaxing views or sounds, save in the sense that, having a certain sensibility, we feel various things to be relaxing. Here then we are drawn to the view that something is relaxing because we find it so. This subjectivist orientation seems the best direction of explanation for a variety of other verdicts regarding the quality of objects of sensuous experience, but what of beauty?

Phenomenologically, beauty seems to reside *in* things: in their form, structure, and texture, in the overall shape, internal arrangement, and medium. Certainly we "feel" the beauty but that feeling is referred toward its object as occasioning the experience. In the case of the relaxing, by contrast, it is more natural to say that we are relaxed by the thing as an effect of it, where it is allowed that others might not be similarly affected. Moreover, in the case of beauty there is the sense that the favorable judgment is *merited* and indeed called for. In identifying something as beautiful one acknowledges its quality as something to be *appreciated*. Furthermore, while judgments of beauty are not governed by rules or sets of criteria, they do have *grounds,* and there is such a thing as aesthetic criticism. While these several points do not put the matter beyond dispute they do, I suggest, provide effective support to the idea that beauty is something real in the world and not just a projection onto it of our sensibility.

What of its extent? Tennant writes that "Nature is sublime or beautiful, and the exceptions do but prove the rule." *Exceptio probat regulam in casibus non exceptis* [that there are exceptions proves the rule in all other cases] warrants an expectation of near to universal conformity to the principle of natural beauty. Considering this, someone is likely to begin with conspicuous and culturally familiar categories: flowers, sunsets, mountains, and so on; and then to start imagining other "parts" of nature to see whether these also conform. Sortal terms divide a domain by kinds, corresponding either to mass or count nouns that attract, respectively, the questions how much? and how many? "Water," unlike "horse," designates a kind that divides into quantities rather than individuals; so that while we may ask "how *many* horses are there?" we can only ask "how *much* water is there?" With this simple semantic apparatus in place, we can now ask whether, for the most part, actual states of affairs properly, and primarily describable in terms of natural sortals exhibit aesthetic qualities. Clouds, mountains, meadows, lakes, rivers, trees, horses, cows, sheep, dogs, cats, fish, algae, can easily be imagined to rest along a scale of the aesthetically pleasing, both in respect of their structure and with regard to their immediately apparent empirical properties. When it comes to quantities of stuffs of various kinds the issue is less clear, but here two things may be said: first, that the thesis of natural beauty holds properly and primarily of things that have some intrinsic principle of unity or organization; and second, that even where something lacks this and is just an aggregation, such as a mound of snow, or a heap of sand, there are other aspects, color, texture, etc, that provide aesthetic interest. As counterexamples suggest themselves, so too does the thought that in saying nature is aesthetic one need not be claiming that all of nature is outstanding, but the deficiencies may be seen as degrees of privation; also where nature is apt to seem repellent that is likely to be because of other non-aesthetic aspects of the situation or of the character of what is contemplated. Again, therefore, I am inclined to think that Tennant's claim stands up.

So we arrive at the two last challenges. Even granting that beauty, or the aesthetic more broadly, is ubiquitous might this not be the product of chance rather than design? A familiar counterpart of that question haunts traditional teleological arguments for the existence of God based on the apparent functional order occurring in nature. For the ancients and mediaevals there was no doubt that the universe exhibits purposeful order, but attempts to draw theological conclusions from this assumption were shown by David Hume to be problematic,[5] and the assumption itself was called into question by Darwin's theory of evolution by natural selection among the products of random variation. Since Hume's challenges are themselves problematic and ambiguous in intent and outcome, and since the Darwinian challenge is directed against the prior claim that nature exhibits purposeful order, and has been the more pressing, here I consider only it.

The first point to be made is that the theory of evolution aims to give a naturalistic explanation of the development of species in terms of the persistence of features that confer advantages on their possessors. It does not exclude the possibility that those features exist by design, but it provides a non-design alternative explanation of them. Strictly this explanation focuses on the adaptive utility of a feature, showing how things possessing it are better equipped to survive and

---

5. See David Hume, "Dialogues Concerning Natural Religion," in *David Hume, Dialogues and Natural History of Religion,* ed. J. C. A. Gaskin (Oxford: Oxford University Press, 1998).

hence to reproduce; but the process of natural selection does not account for the origination of the feature itself, and that fact is left to be explained as a product of random mutation among offspring.

Here is one place where defenders of design arguments may respond. Since it is inconceivable that a heritable adaptive feature could emerge in a single generation, such a feature must be the product of iterative reproduction and cumulative selection. But the regularities required in the mechanisms of replication can themselves hardly be explained as chance products. Otherwise chance is being multiplied many times over into the far outer reaches of improbability. There is something here deserving of attention,[6] but I pass over it now so as to point out that, in any case, the attempt to account for the ubiquity of beauty by evolution through natural selection cannot even get underway. The problem resides in the fact that in order to be "selected for," a feature has to play a causal role in the survival of the organism. Where the natural object in question is not an organism this simply does not apply; and even where it is living, its aesthetic properties cannot intelligibly benefit or disadvantage it.

An exception to the latter case would be where the chances of survival depend upon the predation or support of other organisms. Logically speaking, one could imagine a world where everything natural is beautiful because beautiful things are favored by other creatures, but this is an absurd hypothesis regarding our world, not least because most living things seem indifferent to aesthetic properties, and many of the things whose beauty impresses us, such as mountains and oceans, were formed without significant, if any, contribution from living things. So we are returned to the element of chance without supplement of natural selection, and we have to consider how likely it is that undirected physico-chemical processes could more or less invariably produce aesthetic results. Certainly there is no probability

6. For some further discussion see John Haldane, "Further Reflections on Theism," in J. J. C. Smart and J. J. Haldane, *Atheism and Theism,* 2nd ed. (Oxford: Blackwell, 2003), pp. 223–27.

measure by which to determine this (un)likelihood. More to the point, however, it is barely intelligible to think of events and processes whose causes are not themselves aesthetic, systematically yielding aesthetic effects, and not just "surface finishes" but form and compositional structure. One might speculate that perhaps the processes of natural formation are subject to aesthetic causality immanent within nature itself. That would be to countenance a sort pan-aestheticism, analogous to pan-psychism or pan-vitalism. As a causal hypothesis about the recurrent emergence of beauty, this notion is afflicted with the difficulty that, apart from the mysteriousness of how nature could be like that, it remains obscure how any such process could work. Should we be moved to posit a productive source of beauty in line with the everyday causes with which we are already familiar, namely a designer or artist, then we are brought closer to Tennant's conclusion. Admittedly, such an artist of nature would not yet have been shown to be Divine, but in context and taking account, as Tennant does, of other lines of argument, theism might then appear the best explanation.[7]

There remains, however, one further iteration of the Darwinian theme, not in the effort to account for beauty itself but to interpret our experiences as products of a kind of interest that can be explained without recourse to any aesthetic reality. This iteration conforms to a pattern of reductionist explanation that is currently widely favored among philosophical materialists. Take some feature of human thought and experience judged to be intrinsically important and

7. In addition to the beauty and sublimity of nature Tennant argues (pp. 81–103) from (1) the adaptation of human thought to its object, or the harmony of thought and world; (2) the adaptation of parts to whole in organisms; (3) the adaptation of the inorganic world to the production, maintenance, and development of living things; and (4) the existence and content of morality; for details see his *Philosophical Theology*, vol. II, pp. 81–103. While (2) seems vulnerable to a Darwinian challenge, as may (4); (1) and (3) deserve attention. For efforts in these directions (not related to Tennant's own) see my contributions (sections 2, 4 and 6) to *Atheism and Theism*, supra. For further discussion of Tennant's argument from beauty see Mark Wynn, *God and Goodness: A Natural Theological Perspective* (London: Routledge, 1999), chap. 1.

significant of some aspect of the world. Let it be the sense of moral conscience or, relatedly, that of objective moral demands and prohibitions, or let it be the idea that human life is subject to providence and judgment, or that nature is beautiful. Of themselves, these seem to be real and enduring features of human experience and reflection, not temporary impressions or culturally local phenomena, and they seem to call for an explanation, of which the most direct would be that they are recognitions of objective fact.

If that explanation were correct, then they would indicate realities transcendent of the material world described and accounted for by the natural sciences. Over the centuries, philosophers and theologians have pointed to just such features to argue for the existence of a transcendent domain. Thanks to Darwin and his followers, however, another explanation is available that confines moral, aesthetic and religious experience to the material realm. Assume nothing except life, reproduction, variability and environmental pressures, and a fully sufficient explanation of these subjects is forthcoming. By virtue of the benefits they confer, certain features will be enduringly selected for: psychological stability, co-operative skills, group loyalty, the tendency to internalize advantageous social norms, the propensity to regard the world as well-ordered, and the liability to be at ease with one's natural environment. Given, then, that these dispositions and beliefs confer selectional advantages, it is no surprise that beings who have emerged from generations of environmental and inter-species struggle are possessed of them. Indeed, how could it be otherwise? For animal species that were cognitively ill-adapted in their dealings with the world would not be around to speculate on the fact.

This looks to be an almost irresistible form of explanation, one that promises to sweep away any alternative, and currently it is everywhere to be found: as a species we think, feel, expect, are attracted to, or are repelled by this or that, or hope for or dread such and such, *because* such attitudes either confer selectional advantages or conferred them upon our ancestors long enough for them to settle in our nature. So powerfully illuminating can this explanatory device seem that observers are often frozen in its beam, unable to look away. Yet in form it clearly is quite like the sort of general explanation offered by Marxists, who claim to show that morality and religion are forms of ideological illusion resulting from the unconscious struggle between classes, or by Freud, who seeks to trace them to sexual impulses. But if the explanation has the apparent power of these it also has their real weaknesses. In the present case the claim takes the following form. The appearance to us of beauty and sublimity in nature is to be explained by reference to relationships between our ancestors and the environments in which they evolved, and in the advantages conferred by features of those environments. So, for example, our appreciation of the beauty of hills and wooded landscapes is an ancestral legacy from a time when our forbears hunted in the forests and took advantage of the possibilities of concealment and overview.[8] Creatures sensitive to that sort of terrain fared better, reproduced more extensively, and handed down that sensitivity which somehow along the way transmuted itself into an impression of beauty.

What to say of this? First, in common with many such explanations from evolutionary psychology (as from Marxism and psychoanalysis) it is an untestable, after-the-fact, speculative construction. Second, even if it did provide a sufficient explanation of our experiences (which I am about to dispute), it does not provide a necessary condition for them. This second point might seem an obvious logical one, but in fact the purveyors of these sorts of explanations typically speak as if only their explanation could provide an account of our experiences. But of course there is another and simpler reason why, for example, we seem to see beauty in nature: namely, *that nature exhibits real beauty.* Sophisticated advocates of the reductive alternatives recognize that their position is not logically unique, but they assume that explanations that depend upon the reality of the apparent

---

8. For further (critical) discussion of this approach see John Haldane, "Some Recent Work in Environmental Aesthetics," *Environmental Values* 3, no. 2 (1994): 173–82.

phenomena are to be excluded because the world could not be such as to contain irreducibly aesthetic properties, or moral ones, nor could the universe be such as to intimate a creator. Why not? Because that would be incompatible with materialism. In other words, the reductive explanations are deemed logically sufficient and de facto necessary since their proponents have antecedently excluded reference to values or to a creator. This is somewhat reminiscent of those biblical exegetes who interpret talk of miracles as metaphorical rather than literal, notwithstanding that the literary context appears to be a narrative in which actual suspensions or reversals of nature would be relevant to the situation described and to the task of demonstrating the special nature of the agent. Why? Because they are committed in advance to denying praeternatural efficacy. The technical legal term for such stances is "prejudice," and these are no less cases of it for being advanced by academic authors.

A fair-minded reader might grant this point while yet feeling the pull of the claim that the reductive accounts fully explain the experiences of value, so let me say why they do not. First, I am not excluding (to do so would be prejudicial) the possibility that our relations to the world and to one another are influenced by the environments in which our ancestors lived, or by our sexual natures, or by the economic relations which shaped the past and condition the present; but it is one thing to allow these as framing conditions and another to think that they explain the interior of what is framed. Second, and following on from this, if such factors play a role, it is in directing attention, not in structuring the detail of what is seen. Third, they do not provide norms of critical assessment. Suppose that our liking for wooded hillsides owes something to our ancestors' hunting practices; how does that fact explain the differences in response to a variety of forested landscapes which from the point of view of hunting interest are equivalent. Suppose I say of some river valley scene that it is especially engaging for the way in which the rising skyline of the tree tops establishes a dramatic contrast with the plunging incline of the ground toward the river; or that the olive green of the ground is high-lighted by the dark tones of timber and canopy; and that the stability of the earth is accentuated by the ever-changing waters of the river; and so on. How is this detailed critical appreciation informed, let alone explained, by the claim that this sort of landscape was useful to my distant hunter-gatherer ancestors in their efforts to see without being seen? The question is rhetorical and stands as a challenge to the reductionist. Until such time as he or she provides an intelligible answer we have reason to stand by the initial reasoning that, on the basis of our seeming experience of beauty in nature, we should take it that indeed nature is beautiful; furthermore, that being the case and other explanations of this appearance having been set aside as wanting, we also have reason to attribute this beauty, as in the case of an artwork, to a creator-designer.

III

That philosophical argument could have brought us to this conclusion might be expected to be welcome to a religious believer for whom the material world is regarded as an artefact of God. One might expect that, like Hopkins, and like many an artist and poet before him, such a person would rejoice both in beauty and in reasoning to the effect that the aesthetic in nature points to a divine artist. In fact, however, there is a line of thought that also goes back to Greek antiquity and to early Christianity, according to which the beauty of nature is something from which to avert one's gaze as from a vain distraction. Writing in 1336 to an Augustinian teacher of theology, Francesco Diognigi da Borgo San Seplolcro, Francesco Petrarca famously describes an ascent of Mont Ventoux, the "giant" of Provence, named after Vintur, a Gaulish mountain deity. The idea of ascending to the summit was inspired by a passage in Livy's *History of Rome*. He writes:

> I finally sat down in a valley and transferred my winged thoughts from things corporeal to the immaterial . . . While I was thus dividing

my thoughts, now turning my attention to some terrestrial object that lay before me, now raising my soul, as I had done my body, to higher planes, it occurred to me to look into my copy of St. Augustine's *Confessions*. . . . [and] where I first fixed my eyes it was written: "And men go about to wonder at the heights of the mountains, and the mighty waves of the sea, and the wide sweep of rivers, and the circuit of the ocean, and the revolution of the stars, but themselves they consider not." I was abashed [and] closed the book, angry with myself that I should still be admiring earthly things who might long ago have learned from even the pagan philosophers that nothing is wonderful but the soul, which, when great itself, finds nothing great outside itself. . . . How earnestly should we strive, not to stand on mountaintops, but to trample beneath us those appetites which spring from earthly impulses.[9]

In an age unaccustomed to subjecting pleasures taken in nature to a higher standard of experience and reflection, this passage can seem shocking. Admittedly, Petrarca is not denying the grandeur or the beauty of the mountain landscape, but he is setting against it something held to be not only more profound, but distinctly and incomparably more important, namely, one's soul and the state of it. Part of the difficulty a present-day reader is likely to have in appreciating Petrarca's reaction is not so much the measure of the comparison but the very terms of it.

On the one side there is the vivid aesthetic experience of the beauty and sublimity of the material world, but on the other stands—what exactly? The sense, or rather the idea—since the mode of cognition seems intellectual rather than empirical—of an inner spiritual world within which we discover our "soul," is perplexing. How can an experience of beauty be compared with a thought about the subject of moral, intellectual, and spiritual life? To the extent that the latter is

9. Francesco Petrarca, "The Ascent of Mont Ventoux," trans. Hans Nachod, in Cassirer et al., eds., *The Renaissance Philosophy of Man* (Chicago: University of Chicago Press, 1948), pp. 44–45.

not dismissed as obscurely (or impossibly) metaphysical, it remains puzzling as to why there should be any contest between these. After all, could someone not seek and find beauty in nature, and also seek and achieve spiritual elevation?

Behind Petrarca's observations there is, of course, an implied conflict of orientations and an assumption about where proceeding along those directions would take one. To be concerned with nature is to focus oneself on the material world in an understanding of that realm that might be shared by a pagan, or a materialist, philosopher. The world in that understanding is without spiritual significance. On the other hand, to be concerned with the soul is to direct one's attention to a spiritual domain as first discerned by the idealist philosophers of antiquity (most effectively by Plato) but seen more clearly through the disclosing lens of Christianity (as ground by Augustine). The soul and the spiritual in this understanding are without material composition or character.

Yet while soul and world may be distinct, they are, in the human, (somehow) connected, and the problem is that the material element drags down the spiritual one, pulling it further away from its proper domain to a point where it loses sight of it, and then even interest in it—by which one point one is spiritually dead. The dualism that is increasingly explicit in this interpretation has several aspects. One is the familiar duality of body and soul. It is with eyes of the former that Petrarca looks around and beyond the mountain. But beyond a separation of soul and body lie other dualisms and perhaps a pathological legacy of the Fall including the sense that the material world, even as it reaches skyward, somehow remains a subterranean location set below the spiritual domain, with natural beauty and light being at best reflections of heavenly glory and illumination but, more likely, seductive distractions from them. No reflective celebration of the beauty of nature can proceed without the excavation, and exorcism, of these intellectually primordial oppositions.

IV

The human mind is naturally drawn to a series of dualistic contrasts: exterior and interior, surface and core, visible and concealed, and so on. Although the primary application of these contrasts is physical, they are often reapplied to mark distinctions at the personal and cultural levels; and, though they do not imply it, they are readily adapted to mark instances of the broad distinction between appearance and reality. Likewise, while the idea of the subterranean or underground is evidently a material and spatial concept—whose partner is that of the overground or, more commonly, the surface—it also lends itself to various metaphorical uses.

Most familiar in recent times is the idea of the underground as the place of counter-cultural resistance, particularly to coercively imposed ideologies. The underground seminars and seminaries that sustained independent thought during periods of totalitarian rule are celebrated examples. At the shallower end lie underground or "alternative" forms of contemporary culture. This latter use of the idea of the underground has often been self-congratulatory, inheriting from real cases of clandestine resistance the association of threat and persecution, and including a suggestion of intellectual depth consequent upon lying below the surface.

Interestingly, the idea that underground culture is more serious or more profound—has more integrity, or is closer to truth—than what is formed on the surface in fact reverses the order of things presented in one of the earliest, and still one of the most powerful, imaginative uses of the idea of the subterranean, namely, Plato's allegory of the Cave. This image is introduced in Book IX of the *Republic* (514a) as the third of a series of images (the others being the simile of the Sun and the picture of the Line) by which Plato aims to convey his philosophical views on the nature of knowledge and reality.

Plato has Socrates describe the allegory as providing an analogy for the human condition. He invites the character Glaucon—and, through him, us—to imagine people living from childhood in a deep cavern. At one end of it, far away from where they dwell, is the entrance to a tunnel that slopes slowly up toward an opening to the outside world. The inhabitants are chained with their backs to the direction of the tunnel entrance and facing a near wall of the cave. Some distance behind and parallel to them is low wall with a pathway between it and the entrance. Behind the pathway is a fire, and the light from it projects in front of the cave-dwellers shadows of objects carried along the pathway.

Knowing nothing but these flickering silhouettes, the dwellers take them for reality. Admittedly, it is questionable whether they would describe them as such, since in so limited an environment it is doubtful that they would have framed the contrast between the real and the apparent. Next, though, Socrates asks us to consider what would happen if one of the captives broke free and turned around. Seeing the moving objects and the fire behind, he would soon realize that what he had hitherto taken for real was only a projected shadow world. Reality, he would conclude, is the world of wall, pathway, firelight, passing figures, and the objects they carry.

Suppose, however, that he was then dragged to the tunnel and lead up toward the daylight. Just as when, first turning to the fire, he would be dazzled by the brilliance of the light (but having adjusted to the intensity of illumination he would then make out a new set of objects, the outside world originals of which the carried artefacts were copies), so in turn he would reject these copies as deceptive, and he would identify reality with the surface world. Socrates invites Glaucon to apply the allegory to the actual human condition. What we are ordinarily aware of through the senses corresponds to the shadows and objects of the cave—second- and third-degree appearances—while the outside world corresponds to the true reality of essences—first principles and ultimate causes.

Plato's allegory applies to the general human condition as a whole, but it can be reapplied within that whole to mark degrees of individual and social benightedness and illumination. What is common throughout the *Republic* is the theme of the subterranean as a place of darkness and illusion, and the surface as the domain of the real and the place of enlightenment. In the allegory, illumination comes with a series of movements: turning around, then making the journey to the surface. But what is the non-literal interpretation of this? How are *we* to achieve enlightenment?

Art, philosophy, and religion have all made claims in this regard— sometimes operating singly, sometimes jointly, and sometimes in competition with and even in denial of one another. Art(ifice) featured twice over in the lives of the cave dwellers. The shadows were productions, but so too were the objects that cast them. Even assuming that those objects were modeled on the realities of the surface world, they are at best three-dimensional representations, and the shadows two dimensional silhouettes of those. Plato basis a criticism of art on precisely this gap between the real and its representation, and he makes the case that only philosophy can take us from the world of appearances to the transcendent reality of which it is at best an image.

Something akin to this analysis has lain behind the effort of some conceptual artists to free art-making of any representational medium and to deal directly in ideas. There is, though, something self-defeating in this effort, for all one can do is to substitute one medium of representation for another—rather as if a poet were to denounce in words (what else?) the veiling effect of language. More importantly, however, the analysis deserves to be challenged. Why assume that art can only be a representation of ideas or of extra-mental reality, rather than, say, an expression of them, or a participation in them?

The contrast between what lies beneath and what lies above ground is subject to different completions. In Plato's allegory, nothing of the real appeared underground and only the escapee made the passage from below to above. Yet there is an obvious and vast class of things that are subject to the contrast and yet are not constrained by it. Plants developed from seed or from corms start out beneath the surface and reach down and up in a single unitary form. The spreading root and branch systems express the genotypical blueprints contained in the microbiological structure of the seeds. Here the one reality is both on the surface *and* underground. Furthermore, the nature of the living substance is not an abstract form existing in a super-sensible realm, or an idea held in the mind of a botanical engineer. What lies beneath is not a representation or an effect of what stands above, and neither part is a mere appearance obscuring an invisible reality. The darkness in which the roots develop and draw nourishment is not subordinate to the daylight in which leaves and flowers grow, and these material processes are not secondary to the life of the plant: they are its nature and life.

V

There is an old philosophical slogan: *agere sequitur esse*—acting follows upon being. Put another way: as a thing is, so it does. The nature of living beings is manifest in their characteristic activities, expressed throughout their entire form. Taking this idea and applying it to the case of art, an alternative to Plato's demoting (and demeaning) account suggests itself. Just as a plant does not represent its genetic nature but is an expression of it, so an artwork might aim, not to depict or designate something (an object or idea), but rather to realize a nature, participating in and expressing it. With this possibility in view, conceptual art, in which ideas are given priority over the mode of their expression or representation, is not so much the attainment of unmediated presentation as the evasion of the challenge to create objects whose intrinsic nature, by analogy with the nature of a living organism, is significant and rewarding to contemplate.

This account serves to explain the traditional artistic preoccupation with material and craft. Given the task of designing and making an organism, one would have to think what sort of living thing it would be, and then set about arranging material in ways that realized that form of life. This would be a very material and practical activity—not the intellectual production of an abstract formula, but the engineering of a tangible, functioning self-moving object. So in the making of a piece of art, a form of aesthetic life has to be fashioned through the manipulation of a material medium. Once made, the work lives well or badly according to its design and manufacture.

Ideas are part of art but not a substitute for empirical realities. What eye hath not seen nor ear heard may be the subject of metaphysical or mystical exploration, but it cannot be the literal stuff of art-making. If there is no object (in a suitably [but not indefinitely] broad understanding of what constitutes an object), then there is no artwork: this statement is not a piece of art criticism but a philosophical thesis intended to overcome the dualities discussed earlier. It is intended also to explain why it is that we look for and respond gratefully to well-crafted objects; our search for and satisfaction in them are analogous to those of someone who goes for a walk in the park or in the country and observes various living forms.

Genetic codes are sequences of self-programming data; flora and fauna are the living expression of these codes. Artwork ideas are schemes whose "living" expressions are drawings, sculptures, installations, and so on. However and wherever they originate, however they are composed and constructed, and wherever they are displayed, art works have their roots underground, stabilized in and taking nourishment from some earth somewhere, like the literal soil that includes layers of past forms. In the case of art, though, the foundation into which the seed is planted is always subject to some degree of selection and cultivation. Here too art shows the necessity of craftsmanship.

Having earlier considered and defended the idea that there is an affinity between nature and art, it is interesting to note how these present parallels and analogies prompt the question whether there is any special affinity between art and nature. Certainly many artists have made nature their subject; but much art has not been overtly concerned with nature, and much has opposed itself to nature, not (save in a few cases) as its enemy but as its opposite.

Art being designed and manufactured it is always contrastable with what occurs "by nature"; in itself that is not a very deep or illuminating point. Of course artists may choose anything as their starting points, and work to anything as their conclusion. The question, though, is whether there is something especially fitting in art that, through its subject matter, its form, or its manner of production, engages nature. I suggest that there is, but without implying that such fittingness confers priority or superiority on such work over other art. It is not a matter of prescription or critical assessment; rather it is one of recognizing an affinity. Once we leave behind Plato's image of art as progressively removing us from primary and secondary realities, and when we begin to think instead of embodying and expressing thought and feeling in composed material forms, it is right and fitting to look to nature not only for a philosophical model of the relationship between content and form, but also for content and form themselves.

How that might be pursued is not at all a matter for abstract reflection but is instead a matter for artistic practice, for bringing sensibility and skill to bear in observation, selection, conception, and manufacture. Philosophy may have something to say about what art is, or can be, but no process of conceptual clarification can amount to art-making.

Finally, there is in Plato's allegory of the Cave something worth carrying over to the purposes and practice of art. This is the possibility of discovering the true meaning of things, not by dissecting them, but by seeing them in their context for what they are, and by seeing also that there may be more than one context, and more than one kind of thing. Plato was concerned with the possibilities of transcendence, and art can share in that search for transcendence by exploring the potential of material forms to point toward and perhaps embody further meanings. Whether one chooses to describe those meanings as deeper or higher does not matter, once it is realized that the underground can be a place of revelation as well as one of concealment.

VI

To this point in my discussion, philosophy and literature have been dominant. Finally, and all too briefly, I turn to visual artists' engagement with nature, and here I confine myself to the contemporary, confident that readers need no persuading of the interest and importance of Nicolas Poussin and of Claude Lorrain in the French tradition, of Constable and of Turner in the English, and of Thomas Cole and Frederic Church in the American. In the lectures and book that initiated the contemporary study of landscape in western art— Kenneth Clark's Slade Lectures, entitled *Landscape into Art*[10]—Clark makes the point that in the ancient and medieval worlds there was no such genre as landscape painting; he notes that it was really only in the nineteenth century that this became a dominant form of art-making with its own distinctive aesthetic. Clearly, whatever the effect of material circumstances, these facts are to be explained primarily in terms of changing conceptions of the world (and of the place of human beings within it) and of associated schemes and rankings of values. Accordingly, any attempt to make sense of the nature of landscape art is likely to be something of an exercise in the history of ideas or in conceptual geography rather than a simple chronicle of painting.

One might suppose, therefore, that Clark's assumption that there was "a fairly simple relationship between 'landscape', mean[ing] a good view of a stretch of countryside, while 'art' was what happened to that landscape when it was translated into a painted image . . . landscape was the raw material waiting to be processed by the artist,"[11] was naïve. In fact, however, though he carries his immense learning lightly, Clark is equally well aware of the philosophical complexities of the subject. Not only does he not suppose that the idea of landscape is a conceptual primitive but had he the opportunity he would

10. Kenneth Clark, *Landscape into Art* (London: John Murray, 1949).
11. Ibid., p. 34.

be disposed (and certainly his account has the resources) to reject the assumption that "land" is the basic category. Like the ancients and mediaevals, Clark's preferred starting point is *nature:*

> the concept of landscape changes from things to impressions. Man first shows his consciousness of nature when his art is still symbolic. . . . Flowers, leaves, individual trees, are all "things" which can be thought of in isolation . . . from these individual elements the first landscapes are put together.[12]

For all that Clark sought to interpret the themes of nature and landscape for his own period, these subjects are (regrettably) now of little interest to a rising generation of artists who have next to no experience of rural nature and whose conception of landscape is largely shaped by and confined to the built urban environment. One of the most striking, yet largely unremarked, features of contemporary art is its neglect of landscape. Admittedly there is in Britain and to a lesser extent in North America an educated interest in what might be termed "nature craft," as represented in Britain by artists such as Andy Goldsworthy[13] and Chris Drury.[14] However, this work is more object rather than landscape focused; and whatever its intention, its appeal is largely decorative, hence its presentation in coffee-table style publications. The considerable success of Goldsworthy's work testifies to public appreciation of inventive crafting with natural materials. Other British artists, including David Nash[15] and Peter Randall Page,[16]

12. Ibid., p. 229.

13. See, for example, *Andy Goldsworthy: A Collaboration with Nature* (New York: Abrams, 1990), and Andy Goldsworthy and Terry Friedman, *Hand to Earth: Andy Goldsworth Sculpture 1976–1990* (New York: Abrams, 1993).

14. See Chris Drury, *Chris Drury: Found Moments in Time and Space* (New York: Abrams, 1998), and Chris Drury and Kay Syrad, *Chris Drury* (London: Thames and Hudson, 2004).

15. See Julian Andrews, *The Sculpture of David Nash* (Berkeley: University of California Press, 1999).

16. See Clive Adams, ed., *Peter Randall-Page: Sculpture and Drawing 1977–1992* (London: Randall-Page, 2003).

represent related strands of nature-oriented art. Although more traditionally sculptural in formalism and in materials, their work exhibits the same interest in highly aesthetic surfaces and, once again, it has a greater following outside professional art than within it. By contrast, Roger Ackling's sun drawings, produced by using a magnifying lens to burn lines into a surface, are not well known beyond the art world, though they might easily secure wider interest as poetic delicacies, as they could feed the same appetite for well-crafted artefacts made from natural materials.[17]

Abstracting from the differences between these and similar artists, one might say that their works celebrate the aesthetic delight of natural forms and textures presented through the medium of middle- to small-sized objects. In that sense these works are in continuity with certain fashions in craft and gardening. I suspect this fact partly explains the absence of interest in nature among the avant-garde of the last twenty years: their agendas have been ones of political, cultural, and art-institutional analysis and criticism, whose relevant ideas and values stand at some distance from—if not in opposition to—those of domesticated nature craft. It is all the more interesting, therefore, that the British avant-garde of the late 1960s and early 1970s included artists who turned to nature, landscape, and solitary travel in a spirit of opposition to prevailing art values, and without any irony. (In this regard the British "land artists" are quite unlike their U.S. contemporaries such as Robert Smithson and Michael Heizer, for whose monumental earth displacements the term "land art" was first used.)[18] I have in mind particularly Hamish Fulton and Richard Long, who are largely alone among contemporary artists in being travelers from

17. See Kirsten Glass, *Roger Ackling—Set Aside* (London: Annely Juda, 1998), and John Haldane, "The Art of Roger Ackling," in *Roger Ackling* (St. Andrews: Crawford Arts Centre, 2004).

18. For a general introduction to and survey of the field, see Jeffrey Kastner and Brian Wallis, *Land and Environmental Art* (London: Phaidon, 1998); for a shorter introduction, but one that gives greater emphasis to the more intimate British tradition, see Ben Tufnell, *Land Art* (London: Tate, 2006).

urban culture into the natural landscape and in making their jour-
neys an essential part of their art.[19]

Aside from the fact that other interests and influences have arisen
in the last forty years such as feminism, gender theory, post-structur-
alism, media/music culture, etc., which have no obvious link with the
natural world and also engender suspicion of contemplative detach-
ment, the neglect of landscape may be due to the fact that contemporary artists can see no way of representing it other than by traditional
methods, and no way of relating themselves to it non-ironically.

These conditions represent the burdens of art in a time of obsessive
self-consciousness and alienation not only from the world of nature
surrounding us but also from our internal human nature. Like Petrarca, the contemporary artist has difficulty trusting to his spontaneous
feelings, for in the background stand theories that deem such feelings
to be culturally decadent, or else by-products of our animal past. What
would seem to be called for, therefore, is a second innocence—ap-
proaching nature, not as if one knew nothing about its material structure or about the various influences upon human consciousness, but
letting that knowledge recede into the background rather than stand
in the foreground as a barrier between sensibility and world. Allowing
for what science tells us about the composition of nature, and about
our own ancient history, the fact remains that the natural world presents itself as beautiful, and it does so more in the unpredictable manner of an artwork than in the calculable mode of a mechanism. Gerard
Manley Hopkins combines an insight into what nature shows of Divinity with an understanding of how that showing is obliterated by human industry. Ours is a period in which there is an imperative to undo
the effects of the treading of generations by which all has been seared,

19. For essay-length examinations of the work of Long and Fulton see, respectively,
John Haldane, "In the Nature of Things," *Modern Painters,* vol. X, no. 2 (Summer 1997),
pp. 52–54, and "Images after the Fact," *Modern Painters,* vol. XI, no. 3, Autumn 1998,
pp. 92–95. For longer studies see R. H. Fuchs, *Richard Long* (London: Thames and Hudson, 1986); Anne Seymour, *Richard Long: Walking in Circles* (London: Thames and
Hudson, 1991); and Ben Tufnell, *Hamish Fulton: Walking Artist* (London: Tate, 2002).

bleared, and smeared, and once again, though shod, foot is feeling soil. On that account one may anticipate the prospect that, as in the past, artists and through them the culture more generally will come to reconnect with the beauty of nature, seeing in it something to be savored and not eschewed, and in doing so we may rediscover the route that leads onward to the recognition that the world is charged with the grandeur of God.[20]

20. The writing of this paper was made possible by research support provided by the Institute for the Psychological Sciences. I am particularly grateful to Dr. Gladys Sweeney, Dean of the Institute, for facilitating this support.

two

~

Carroll William Westfall

CHRISTIANITY AND ARCHITECTURE,

ARCHITECTURE AND CHRISTIANITY

The epistle read for the second Sunday of Lent in the Episcopal
Church where I worship and have my membership was from St. Paul's
letter to the Philippians at 3:17–21:

> Brothers and sisters, join in imitating me, and observe those who live
> according to the example you have in us. For many live as enemies of
> the cross of Christ; . . . Their end is destruction; their god is the bel-
> ly; and their glory is in their shame; their minds are set on earthly
> things. But our citizenship is in heaven, and it is from there that we
> are expecting a Savior, the Lord Jesus Christ. He will transform the
> body of our humiliation that it may be conformed to the body of his

I should like to acknowledge the assistance derived from the close reading and
suggestions of Samir Younés and David Gobel.

48

glory, by the power that also enables him to make all things subject to himself.

This is a fitting introduction for my huge topic, which is not Christian architecture, that is, architecture specifically in the service of the religious rites and practices of Christian religion. Rather, it is the interaction between Christianity and architecture, and, more specifically, the effect Christianity has had on architecture.

My use of the term Christianity follows that of the *Catholic Encyclopedia*:

> [A] supernatural religion and the only absolute one; ... instituted by God in the fullness of time, and containing a revelation of Himself, which all to whom it has been adequately presented are bound under pain of eternal loss to accept [I call particular attention to that statement; I'll come back to it at the end] ...; enabling human nature to rise to the sublimest heights and "to play the immortal"; ... the one bond of civilization, the one condition of progress, the one hope of humanity ... the Church of Christ, the "city set upon a hill", conspicuous ... through the notes that proclaim her Divine.... It ... makes evident how real is human liberty and how grave human responsibility.[1]

An important aspect of that definition is the implicit claim that Christianity has an institutional structure that claims the authority to define doctrine based on interpretations of revelation, an authority that reaches into both the sacred and the secular worlds.

Architecture is a natural ally of such an institution because by its very nature it is a public art that comes into being through the actions of the institutions and officials who have the power and resources to build. It therefore serves its builders not only by accommodating their needs but also by representing what they want it to represent.

This alliance between authoritative institutions and buildings endowed architecture with a much greater representational power than

1. Joseph Keating, "Christianity," in *The Catholic Encyclopedia*, New York (Robert Appleton: 1908), s.v. Christianity, vol. III, pp. 712–20, p. 720.

we are accustomed to expecting from it. Traditionally, a building serving an institution has been distinguished from one serving mere utility by being vested with a higher level of architectural achievement, one that gives it a beauty appropriate to the moral purpose of the institution it serves. Today, in an age dominated by modernism in architecture, such an alliance between institutions and buildings is largely absent. Instead of being thought of as parts of a hierarchically ordered urban and rural realm serving a coherent civil or religious institutional order, a building's importance is reduced to something much simpler, and more simplistic. Each new building is a new phenomenon, being simply a means by which its builder, whether architect or client, expresses himself, and the formal content used to do so yields little more insight than a few adjectives can convey. For example, a big building represents big ambitions, a small one more humble ones, an odd one represents "creativity," and a traditional one stability or a failure to get with the times.

Traditionally, architecture has made available two deeper layers of representation, particularly among buildings serving religion. One layer allows a building to signify something else. That is, a building or a part of a building looks like something else, and that resemblance conveys some sort of meaning. For example, making a column shaft look like a tree trunk makes clear the origin of the column in a tree and the necessity of using artifice and craftsmanship to move it from nature to culture. Similarly, making a column in the form of a human body, even abstracted to one of the traditional, canonic columnar orders with a base, shaft, and capital, signifies the anthropomorphic analogy that likens the form of a building to the form of a human body (see Figure 1). I will give some reasons for doing this later. In like manner, that the federal government and a state government are two entities of a common polity is made explicit by deriving the form for a state capitol from that of the United States Capitol.

The other, and more abstract, means of representing is *symbolically*. A symbol makes visible something that is otherwise invisible.

Figure 1. The tree, the human form, and the Tuscan order in close juxtaposition at Thomas Jefferson's University of Virginia, Charlottesville, Virginia, from 1822–26. The first two are products of nature, the third a product of culture that makes visible the best aspects of nature's formal properties and the order, proportion, and coherence that underlie their form. *(Photograph by author)*

The light within a Gothic church symbolizes the illumination available through revelation; the dome of a Renaissance church symbolizes the universality and order of the cosmos within which God spreads his grace. The grounding of justice in our polity in the same enduring principles that have guided other polities that aspire to justice is symbolized by basing the design of a courthouse, for example the one from 1836 in Palmyra, Virginia, on a Greek temple, which also calls to mind that court house's superior institutional structure, Thomas Jefferson's Virginia Capitol in Richmond, designed almost fifty years earlier.

Both significant and symbolic content require using conventions within a common tradition. The content is rendered through architectural form, not through duplication or replication of the appearance of the thing to which it refers. That is, the content takes on forms that belong to the art of architecture. To be effective in serving the institutions that bring buildings into being, the principles giving order to that transformation of content into architectural form must have the same origin as the principles used to give order to the institutions the building serve. Otherwise, the building is less than architecture. It is mere construction.

Thus far we have seen that architecture requires the patronage of an authoritative institution, which it serves and represents, and that buildings convey meaning on behalf of that institution. Finally, architecture does one more thing: it defines the extent of the reach of the authority it serves and represents. Another way to say all this is to note that politics is more important than architecture and that buildings represent authoritative institutions and officials not only by their material, physical presence but also by their embodiment of an interpretation of man's place in the universe of nature.

With this understanding of Christianity and of architecture in mind, let me present some thoughts about the effect Christianity has had on the art of architecture. The effect has been positive, and it consists of four contributions.

Christianity's first contribution to architecture was to make it normative that buildings include an axial sequence of interior spaces that are significant in themselves and that are intended to accommodate the activities of all people who find these activities significant.

Architecture was a mature art before Christ was born. It had its earliest complete embodiment in Egypt in the third dynasty around 2600 BC at the funerary complex of the Pharaoh Zoser in Saqqara. Zoser's tomb extends the burial cavern upward into a stack of mastabas to become the first pyramid, this one a stepped affair with tapered sides that others later on would recalibrate and smooth out to produce the familiar pyramid form. This huge burial mound dominated a precinct holding various storehouses, courtyards, and hypostyle halls containing all that the pharaonic household needed for the journey to the afterlife. That it was built in cut stone, the earliest known instance of this technique, demonstrates the desire for permanence and command over the highest technology. The storehouses and some other buildings are full, but full of stone and not of grain, just as all but one of the many gates leading into the precinct are blind, that is, lacking openings. Why? Because this removes them from material reality and elevates them into the higher reality conveyed by fiction. For the same reason the columns, including those that are attached to walls, are stone but composed to look like bundled reeds and lotus. Within the precinct, the buildings and open areas are ordered into a studied relationship to one another. Fundamental to the complex's organization is a series of interior, roofed spaces aligned along an axis with chambers diminishing in size as the number of people permitted to enter them becomes ever more restricted. The order within the complex stops at the walls; the area within models the universe, the area outside is chaos. This precinct, which was built to provide an afterlife for the pharaoh, is the product of the art of a person, an architect named Imhotep, the first architect whose name we know. Imhotep also commanded other arts, and would eventually be deified as a physician (the Greeks knew him as Asclepius). At Saqqara he brought together and coordinated into a single design all the components of architecture: significant and symbolic content serving an institution and rendered with artful fiction within an artfully constructed and impressive actual, material place, accomplished with high technology, done by means of architecture's imitation of the ordering principles of the cosmos, and arising from the skill and knowledge of an architect.

At Saqqara, Imhotep and Zoser sought to protect the eternal order of the pharaoh's precinct from the chaos of change lying outside the walls. Christianity is one of the religions that accepts no such segregation of the unchanging from the changing. Christianity, which is our concern here, knows that men live in a world marked by the change known as history that unfolds within the eternal cosmos governed by God's divine providence. As a religion existing in historical time, Christianity knows the world as a dynamic interplay between the flux of change and the unchanging truths about God's presence in His creation. We cannot know the divine order of things completely in this life, but we have access to it through revelation, reason, and tradition. This epistemology synthesizes contributions from Jerusalem, Athens, and Rome, just as the architecture that would serve it did.

Egyptian architecture had sought to preserve a static world. The Greeks transformed architecture to address a dynamic one. They invented the paradigmatic conventional model for all subsequent architecture in the West, the Greek temple form, which in its parts and their assemblage makes visible current knowledge about the interplay between the enduring and the changing. In so doing, its material imitates and manifests the form of the actions arising from the relationships of the citizens to one another, to the gods, and to the cosmos, actions that define the polis. The temple is, therefore, a counterpart to the polis, and it is its material, visible model.[2]

But the reach of the order that that architecture claims on the world is no farther than the limits of the temple's fane, the precinct set aside as sacred to its god. Just as at Saqqara the static order within the complex stops at the walls, so the order of the cosmos made visible in the order, proportions, and commensurability of the Greek temple did not project beyond the sacred precincts. The things the Hellenic Greeks built to serve quotidian, mundane activities, including the quite serious business of conducting the affairs of their polis, had no claim on the enduring, and they were built without architects and made no claim to making the cosmic order visible.[3]

The Romans added civil and domestic structures to the category

2. For the actions of the polis and the citizen, see Leo Strauss, *The City and Man* (Chicago and London: University of Chicago Press, 1964); for the conventional forms of the temple as their material embodiment, see Indra Kagis McEwen, *Socrates' Ancestor: An Essay on Architectural Beginnings* (Cambridge and London: MIT Press, 1994).

3. There are a few minor exceptions to this statement, but the comparison is stark when the Hellenic age is juxtaposed against the Hellensitic, the time when serious

of buildings deserving the attention of architects. During their flourishing under the emperors, they invented ways to make impressive interiors for their baths, basilicas, temples, and palaces. They also contrived ways to make the areas open to the sky in their fora, baths, theaters, and stadia as important as the roofed ones. Each one of their buildings imitated the cosmic order, and purely religious structures dominated the hierarchy of buildings, but each building was nonetheless bounded by the limits of its precinct. None of them claimed universal jurisdiction. The buildings and unroofed precincts produced the urban order serving the Roman civil order. The civil order was a collection of legal relationships between otherwise discrete entities, and so too was the urban order. The glue holding together the civil and the urban order was the arrangement of people and buildings into a hierarchical gradation culminating in the imperial authority, which enjoyed both legal and divine supremacy. Greek cities had been built as a common enterprise, but Roman cities were the products of competition between individuals, or of family clans, who used the patronage of architecture as a means of fulfilling a civic duty and elevating their status in the civil order. Far reaching as the Roman world was, at its base it was parochial.

This was the world in which God came to live among men as Christ. During most of the first three centuries after Christ's life on earth, Christians were forbidden a visible presence as Christians in this civil and urban order. They prudently remained hidden, their needs being satisfied by the building type lowest in status, the *domus,* the seat of the family unit. We will encounter it again later, in a different context.

Once Constantine sanctioned Christianity in the imperial world and allowed it to assume a public presence within the Empire, the Christians could contrive an architecture that represented their new position within the imperial civil and urban order. In architecture as

---

attention was given to the buildings charged with secular affairs even as the previously dynamic conduct of those affairs atrophied.

in philosophy and other cultural fields, they did so by absorbing and transforming existing traditions and conventions, giving them new forms, and investing them with new meanings that absorbed and transformed but did not cancel the old ones.

Constantine signaled Christianity's new status by sponsoring the construction of great churches in Rome and Jerusalem with the two in Rome, St. Peter's and San Giovanni in Laterano, of particular interest to us. The origin of their design was in the paradigmatic pagan urban forum, normally one of the most important products of imperial patronage. As a precinct containing several different buildings, a forum enclosed and embodied a cosmic order. Its basilica was the site of commerce and business and, more importantly, of legal proceedings. And its temple had an altar in front and a cult statue within. The precinct Constantine built at the Tomb of St. Peter, which would be particularly influential, followed this pattern, but Constantine's construction transformed the constituent parts to accord with the model of the Temple in Jerusalem. The Romans had destroyed the second successor to Solomon's Temple in AD 70, two-and-a-half centuries earlier, so it was known only in descriptions. The ritual and symbolic content of buildings is more easily conveyed to new buildings constructed in very different circumstances when the precedents are known only through words, and that was certainly the case here.[4]

Although the component parts would have been familiar from forum and temple precincts of pagan antiquity running all the way back to Saqqara, the arrangement and character in this Christian version

4. Solomon's temple is described in 1 Kgs. 5–7, recapitulated in 2 Chr. 2–7; the circumstances of its rebuilding after the Babylonian exile, with some physical description, are given in Ezra 3–8. There is no biblical description of the third, the largest, built by Herod, of which impressive fragments survive. Among the descriptions Ezekiel's vision (Ezek. 40–44) was the most authoritative. Its kernel outlined the form, disposition, and accommodation to ritual common to all three temples, but it vastly enriched the formal and symbolic content of the other descriptions. See Simon Goldhill, *The Temple of Jerusalem* (Cambridge: Harvard University Press, 2005), which appeared subsequent to the completion of this paper.

of a traditional complex was something new, something that would differentiate it from pagan temples and would bring Solomon's Temple to the minds of the faithful. The parts were arranged in an axial sequence, and all of the enclosed spaces, including the final sacred space, were accessible to all believers. The first element to be encountered was the forecourt and narthex, exterior spaces where communicants completed their ablutions before proceeding and where the catechumens remained until prepared through baptism for full membership in the Church. The next space was the long hall whose design with *a higher central nave* (to use the name Christians gave it) *and lower side aisles* was based on the pagan basilica. The pagan building normally had several entrances and no particular axial emphasis, but the Christian version had a longitudinal axis running from entrance to altar that called to mind the pagan temple's axis culminating in the cult statue. The Christian basilica held the members of the Church who congregated for participation in the liturgies. At its far end was the third space, the sanctuary protecting the relics of the martyrs, Peter principal among them, on whose sacrifice the Church had been founded. The focus of the spatial complex was the altar, originally set in front of the sanctuary but eventually moved back into the sanctuary to produce the arrangement that became normative for Christian churches based on the authority of the See of Peter.

The visibly explicit origins of Constantine's Christian basilicas in the architecture that served the Empire made clear his sponsorship of the Christian faith. Transforming a building used for administering the civil law of the Empire into a Christian church signified that the Church was a place in which justice was dispensed, a justice sanctioned by imperial authority, a justice available to all who sought it. The origin of this Christian justice was divine, as symbolized by the liturgy of the Mass conducted at the altar. The Jewish origins of the holy mysteries of the liturgy were signified by the evocation of the Temple of Jerusalem, and its rebuilding in this new form symbolized the supersession of the doctrine of Christian Grace over Jewish Law.

The Constantinian basilicas were unlike any earlier buildings within the Egyptian, Greco-Roman, or Hebraic traditions. Each of them, in its own way, brought together into an integrated whole an axial arrangement concluding in an interior of interrelated spaces accommodating the activities each was built to serve with the significance of those activities called out by the architectural design serving them. For the first time, an interior space accommodated all those who participated in the rites of religious worship. The whole of the body of Christians had access to the sacred liturgies conducted within the building, although there was a distinction between the several classes of people composing this assembly, which is the Church founded by Christ on the Rock of Peter, the Church that is the body of Christ in this world. We take for granted that the interior of a building serving a public, civil or religious purpose has a sequence of related spaces that are assembled to focus attention on the significance the building has in the lives of those who use it. When a building is otherwise, we know it is a departure from our expectations about architecture, and we seek out the reason for that departure. Establishing this characteristic as normative for architecture was Christianity's first important effect on Western architecture.

Christianity's second contribution to architecture was to invest it with a beauty possessing a content that makes clear the service the building provides in a moral universe.

Christianity's second contribution arose from the significant and symbolic content of that new kind of architecture. Compared to figurative media such as painting and sculpture, architecture's ability to *signify* by pointing to something else that it resembles is limited. The Augustan architect Vitruvius, the only pagan author of a comprehensive treatise on architecture, had noted that things are important not only for themselves but for what they signify. He developed a semiotics on that basis, but its purpose was to make clear the role that the emperor, the ultimate patron of all Roman architecture both secular and sacred, played in governing the order of the world.[5] For obvious reasons, this hardly served the purposes of early Christians.

More fruitful was St. Augustine's conversion of ancient rhetorical practices for use by the Christian preacher. In *On Christian Doctrine*, St. Augustine explained that we can learn significant doctrine though the interpretation of signs, that all signs are things, that we can teach doctrine by using things that signify, and that we are to love the doctrine the signs signify but not the things themselves. Constantine's buildings, like those of the pagans, had used this method of signification, which over time would become richly elaborated to serve the purposes of the Church. Here are two examples: A triumphal arch at the end of a nave or on a façade uses an ancient building type to refer to the triumph of the Christian over death and of the Church of Christ over pagan religion. A temple front on a Christian church signifies the triumph of Christianity over paganism. A cluster of domes or towers makes visible to those living in this world the Heavenly Jerusalem described in the Apocalypse. Clear as these signs are, the figurative arts offered greater clarity and a much richer range of content, and so painting and sculpture ornamenting the building and not essential for the building's architectural character as architecture always carried a greater burden in presenting doctrine.

This signification by architecture, by arch or temple or dome or the like, verges on symbolism, but architecture's ability to *symbolize* is actually a much more complicated matter than signification. It requires merging theology, aesthetic theory, and architectural theory. Again, St. Augustine laid the groundwork for such an aesthetic. When acknowledging that there is beauty in things, he asked "whether these things are beautiful (pulchra) because they delight (delectant), or delight because they are beautiful? . . . [T]hey delight because they are beautiful."[6] And why are they beautiful? Because they symbolize God's love.

5. For this point, see now the important study by Indra Kagis McEwen, *Vitruvius: Writing the Body of Architecture* (Cambridge and London: MIT Press, 2003).

6. *True Religion* (*de vera religione*), trans. Edmund Hill, O.P., in *The Works of Saint*

Formulating an aesthetic in which architecture could symbol-ize God's love required concepts brought into the West by Dionysius the pseudo-Areopagite, a Neoplatonist active two generations after St. Augustine. According to this aesthetic, the physical appearance of a church building can make God's love visible by rendering the in-visible attributes of His grace and love in the proportionate harmo-nies and other qualities that signify the presence of His order. Among these are number, proportionality, and light, which we will enjoy in the Heavenly Jerusalem. Their presence in our vision makes the en-joyment of the beauty of God's creation accessible to the soul. In their fully elaborated form in the hands of St. Thomas Aquinas, these quali-ties were rendered in the terms of integrity (or perfection), propor-tion (or harmony), and clarity (or luminosity), which constitute what has been called the Scholastic aesthetic trilogy.[7]

Medieval Christian aesthetics generally used the word *pulcher* for beauty, as Augustine did in *de vera religione*, the equivalent of the Greek concept *to kallos* that invests visually beautiful things with a moral content. Vitruvius, the pagan theorist, used neither that word nor the concept. His word for the delight a person takes in what he sees in a building is *venustas,* which is a kind of attractiveness or charm, a voluptuous beauty of a mundane sort that was immediate-ly perceptible and resided in the realm of the senses.[8] Vitruvius sug-gested that its presence derives from following the natural laws that conform to precepts of geometry and numerology in philosophy and are observable in the well-formed human body. His passage concern-ing the relationship between the form of the body and the form of a

Augustine: A Translation for the 21st Century, ed. Boniface Ramsey, New City Press (Hyde Park, N.Y.: 2005), Part I, vol. 8, pp. 29–104; §32, ¶59.

7. Władysław Tatarkiewicz, *History of Aesthetics,* ed. C. Barrett, vol. II: *Medieval Aesthetics* (The Hague, Paris: Mouton; Warsaw: PWN-Polish Scientific Publishers, 1970), II, p. 253.

8. McEwen, *Vitruvius,* p. 200, where the word is discussed in conjunction with *pulcher,* pulchritude, discussed also infra.

building becomes the *locus classicus* for this anthropomorphic analogy that is central to ancient Greek and Roman architecture, a role it continued to play in the revisions that Renaissance Christians would make to ancient learning. But his ideas about *venustas* were less useful because *venustas* is a very limited kind of beauty. It provides pleasure and it links buildings to principles of nature, but it has no moral content, it does not address the soul, and it does not make visible the invisible mystery of God's role in His creation.

These limitations rendered his treatise inadequate for an architecture serving Christianity. It fell into desuetude as a guide for architects, just as the role of architect did. In the place of the architecture antiquity had developed, a manner of building *was developed* that exploited the symbolic content available in the trilogy of integrity, proportion, and clarity. The beauty that that trilogy made manifest could symbolize God's presence within the city of man, thereby making the City of God present within the city of man. This way of building furnished Christianity an energetic architecture that depended upon another Scholastic innovation, the recognition that the interplay between the building and the viewer allowed the building's beauty to reveal the presence of God. As we know from visiting medieval churches, this is a very appealing beauty. In an age of rapidly expanding commercial prosperity, characteristic of the two-and-a-half centuries after 1100, bishops, various monastic leaders, popes, kings, emperors, other imperial officials, and free communes—that is, virtually all those who enjoyed positions of authority in the earthly cities of man—eagerly sponsored the construction of cathedrals and other churches that provided radiant, stirring, moving examples of their loving support for the City of God in their midst. But various monastic communities, most famously the Cistercians, fearful that people would love the things that were visible rather than the invisible significance they were meant to convey, looked askance at such displays of worldly beauty. The buildings and fittings they produced were known more for their spareness than for their richness. Both approaches, different as they were, produced beautiful results, equally appealing yet distinctly different.

Beauty comes in many forms. Whether a sensuously rich beauty was rejected because it might be enjoyed for its own sake, or such a beauty was thought necessary to honor a rich God, buildings and their fittings were to provide an earthly equivalent to the beauty of God and the moral universe He made. In Scholastic and then in early Renaissance aesthetics (or theology), beauty of this sort, as the visible presence of the universe's moral content, became the principal criterion for judging architecture. Investing architecture with beauty of this sort, that is, with a content that makes clear its role in a moral universe, was Christianity's second contribution to architecture.

Christianity's third contribution to architecture was to include within the office of the architect responsibility for his own moral well-being and for that of his fellow citizens.

The third contribution concerns the role of the architect in society. From Imhotep onward, the architect worked with others to achieve the ends sought by the community in which he lived and worked. Pagan communities, including the Roman city, were always partial, tribal, and exclusionist, and their law did not participate in the eternal law of God. Christianity acknowledged this by pointing out that during their sojourn on earth, people will be citizens of cities such as these, but it also made available citizenship within the City of God to all who believe. With the advent of the City of God within the city of man, citizenship became universal in a way that it was not for pagans. St. Paul put it this way: "For in one spirit we are all baptized into one body—Jews and Greeks, slaves or free—and we are all made to drink of one Spirit" (1 Cor. 12:13).

Implicit in this doctrine is the idea that the duty of the architect is to build the city of man to host and serve the City of God. The challenge implicit in this idea led to the development of the modern concept of the architect, a concept that extended to a new understanding of the city, one in which the intersection of the city of man and the City of God became a concrete, material reality. Meanwhile, similar momentous developments were foot in other fields in Italy. Increased wealth supported new interests ranging from civic and religious building enterprises, the acquisition of texts that had been largely unstudied for a thousand years, and the support of scholars who extracted from the texts new insights into ancient knowledge. Innovative ideas in political theory were developed in states and cities that conducted a robust disputation on whether the justice provided by a republican government had the same authority as the justice dispensed by the officers of the traditional imperial structure. Machiavelli, monarchs of newly formed nation states, and, eventually, the English and American revolutionaries would draw on these ideas. In 1420 the turmoil within the Church brought on by the Schism and the Babylonian Captivity was stilled when Pope Martin V returned to Rome. The Church's tranquility was now roiled principally by a lively debate concerning whether the Pope or a Council should have greater authority in defining doctrine and governing its secular and sacred affairs. With Luther, the Reformation, and the Counter Reformation pushing this argument to extremes, the discussion could no longer be contained within the Church, and the body of Christ would be threatened with dismemberment.

This was the setting within which ideas that had an earlier origin were developed. We might take as their starting point the 1290s when the newly established republican regime in Florence began building a new, very large city hall and a new, huge cathedral that together would signify how these republicans could provide justice in the city of man and properly host the City of God. A hundred twenty years later, the city hall, equipped with a piazza specially cleared to show it off, presented a commanding presence in the city, but the cathedral, also visible across areas calculated to focus one's attention at it, still lacked its dome. In 1417 construction leading to its completion was begun, following the competition-winning proposal of Filippo Brunelleschi. Twenty years later, work was completed on a cupola that was as wide as the dome of the ancient Pantheon in Rome but perched high in the air above the cathedral's altar. Its completion was cited as proof that nature had not grown old and incapable of producing geniuses who could accomplish such feats.

Brunelleschi's genius manifested itself in two other important achievements. One of these was to provide the definition of the architect. When directing the dome's construction he demanded that his role be recognized as the work of the head and not of the hands. He based his unprecedented claim on the criteria Vitruvius had set out, but as we have seen, the ancient concept of the architect had fallen into desuetude during the Middle Ages. Now that the *venustas* that Vitruvius sought in architecture was supplemented by a morally laden concept of beauty, the architect could be brought back into service. The beauty of God's love that an architect could make visible in a building would move people to seek the good. This was the parallel in architecture to the task of preaching that Petrarch, following St. Augustine, had formulated and broadcast in the years just before Brunelleschi, the first modern architect, was born. The buildings the architect designed were now known to be products of the head and to be laden with moral content.

The second achievement concerned making the dome's beauty enjoyable not only for its own sake but also as a visible symbol of the invisible offer of Grace available through the Church. Brunelleschi did this by forcing people to acknowledge the relationship they had to the significant content of the buildings serving the authoritative institutions in their lives. As the late Norris Kelly Smith argued, Brunelleschi invented perspective to accomplish that purpose.

Perspective is a geometrical and mathematical technique for rendering three-dimensional solids and voids on a two-dimensional surface. It is the way a camera sees the world. Brunelleschi demonstrated the two variations of the technique with a pair of panels, both now lost. Following his demonstration, perspective quickly became standard in artistic practice and remained unchallenged until the late nineteenth century, when Impressionist painters found a way to dissolve the material certainty of the world they painted. Their innovations were followed by cubism in the early twentieth century which artists invented as a way to present a world based solely on their own imagining.[9]

Brunelleschi's panels gave a new urgency to the meaning borne by the things they presented to vision. The first panel simulated placing the person in the doorway of the new Cathedral and having him gaze directly at the Baptistery. Here he looks squarely at the portal to the City of God. The second one placed the person at the precise point in the city where, after crossing Florence from the Baptistery and Cathedral, he can first see the City Hall. If in the first one he looks squarely at the City of God, here he confronts the city of man. All the buildings in the panels were in the same scale relationship and reproduced their actual spatial relationships to one another and to the sky and therefore to the universe in all of its changing aspects. They presented an orderly facsimile of the world within which the viewer would lead his life as a Christian and as a citizen. The panels forced on the viewer this query: I occupy a place, a particular place, in this quite material, quite tangible world. What am I to do in this world within the order available through these institutions?

The dome, the claim of intellectual status for the architect, and the invention and demonstration of the panels are a package. Brunelleschi's interventions in the material, visible world addressed the moral well-being of his fellow citizens. Success would earn him heavenly glory from which, as Petrarch explained, would follow earthly fame. This is in marked contrast with Vitruvius's position. He had explained that the architect's office was to serve a patron who sought fame and glory through the architect's work. Whatever fame the architect received

9. See Norris Kelly Smith, *Here I Stand: Perspective from Another Point of View* (New York: Columbia University Press, 1994).

came as a reflection of his patron's fame. He did not act according to his own will as a moral agent but as an extension of his patron's will. While the buildings he produced modeled the universe, it was not a moral universe. And, while buildings offered *venustas,* Vitruvius was, as we saw, silent about morally laden beauty.

In reformulating the office of the architect to include responsibility for his own moral well-being and for that of his fellow citizens, Brunelleschi had produced Christianity's third contribution to architecture.

Christianity's fourth and final contribution to architecture was to define the architect's role to be that of imitating God's work of creation as he builds in the world.

The fourth contribution is closely related to the third. To define it I must take a slightly roundabout route.

Brunelleschi's contribution to architecture was acknowledged and expanded in a treatise on architecture that embedded these ideas in the larger universe of learned discourse and knowledge. Its author was another Florentine, Leon Battista Alberti (1404–72), an intellectual trained in the law who entered the priesthood and served in the papal curia. Alberti preceded his treatise on architecture with one on painting in which he gave an explanation of the theory supporting Brunelleschi's invention of perspective, integrating it with ancient and Augustinian rhetorical practices. The result would be paintings with rhetorical sting that could move viewers to piety and virtuous conduct. Then, using Vitruvius's treatise as his scaffolding, he applied these ideas to architecture; he wrote, however as a humanist interested in making ancient tradition and knowledge useful in the present rather than as a theologian applying Christian doctrine to architecture.

The base of that scaffolding was the trilogy that Vitruvius used for assessing buildings. It is today perhaps the best known and most familiar basis for architectural criticism. Well-building, as Vitruvius's words come out in the seventeenth-century English rendition, consists in commodity, firmness, and delight (*venustas*). These are the conditions a building must satisfy if it is to be good as the product of construction. They make a good *building*, but they do not satisfy the more demanding criteria of *architecture*. They are necessary but not sufficient for architecture. Something more is required for the building to reach the higher level of the scaffold supporting architecture. Vitruvius lists symmetria, eurythmia, and *decor* as three criteria that find a new role to play in Alberti's theory of architecture.

Alberti accepted from Vitruvius the necessary conditions of commodity, firmness, and delight, but he transformed the next level, the criteria of symmetria, eurythmia, and *decor*, into a more inclusive set of criteria. In so doing, he brought the Scholastic concept of beauty and Brunelleschi's invention of perspective into architectural theory. The first of his criteria, which he calls numbering, acknowledges that a building is constructed from a number of different parts—for example doors and windows serving as openings, piers and columns serving as supports, and so on—and this criterion seeks to assure that the building is composed of a proper number of these parts. His second criterion, outline, bounds the material components, such as stones used for walls, the various parts used to make openings, and columns, with geometric properties that give them symmetry, that is, commensurability within a three-dimensional geometric matrix. Brunelleschi's invention of perspective provided the conceptual framework for this use of geometry to give definitive form to material. The third criterion, collocation, assembles these components into a building that possesses what Vitruvius called proper eurythmia, that is, the proportionate harmonies binding the pieces together in an imitation of the proportionate harmony of the universe God made. Here we find the contribution of medieval aesthetic doctrine. And the fourth is *concinnitas* or concinnity, a word taken from rhetoric and used until recently in English to refer to the harmony, congruity, and consistency of an assemblage. Alberti states that *concinnitas* is the first rule of nature, something she uses in her productions, a quality visible to the senses, and a fundamental quality of the beauty we see in nature's production and in those of the architect. His word for beauty in this context is the morally charged *pulcher.*

A building satisfying the conditions and criteria Alberti presented is a physical, material thing imbued with symbolic meaning, as its medieval predecessor had been, but something utterly unlike its medieval predecessors. Their beauty resided in the proportionality and light that dissolved in the radiant presence of the mysteries they made visible. The symbolic content Alberti would make visible was also contained in proportionality and light, but this was now found principally in the proportions of the material pieces from which the building was made and in the proportionate harmonies and adjustments of their assemblage into a tangible, physical thing, as these are subjected to the disciplined, intellectual control that originates in the architect's interpretation of the enduring principles God uses to create in nature. This was a new kind of thing. It is clear to us when we consider two churches from these two different periods, say, Notre Dame in Paris and St. Peter's Basilica in Rome (although envisage St. Peter's before its current seventeenth-century interior decoration allowed precious materials and figurative art in the form of painting and sculpture to interfere with the vivid apprehension of the purely architectural features of the building). Both serve the Christian religion, but they are as different from one another as medieval Catholicism is from that of the Renaissance.

Furthermore, he presented these buildings as parts of an assemblage that makes a city. The buildings he had in mind as forming the city are not merely the few that were emblematic of the families, the civil government, and the Church that had been adequate for representing a city before he and his colleagues transformed our way of thinking about cities and their buildings. The new list reached out to encompass the entire range of buildings found in a city. People could also now see and understand that the buildings also defined and gave order to the voids between the buildings. Now it became possible to treat both the solids and the voids, both the buildings and the streets and squares, as parts of the same physical, earthy ensemble composing their city. This is the kind of city of which Alberti says the principal beauty is its well-ordered layout. This is the city in which people actually live their earthly lives.

He also stated that the principal beauty of a city is its church. A beautiful church will fill the visitor with piety, fill his soul with religion, and let him know that "what he saw was a place undoubtedly worthy of God."[10]

And finally, he also explained that the principal beauty of a church is in the proper use of properly designed columnar orders.

The columnar orders carry with them the anthropomorphic analogy that likens the form of a thing to the form of man. Vitruvius had rooted his analogy in formal, numerical, and geometric terms. Alberti eschewed the formal, and instead he developed the numerical and geometric analogies. This allowed the anthropomorphic analogy to establish a linkage between man as microcosm in a natural, material world that included man and man's actions in the history in which he works out his fate. God is the author of this natural world, the world He created and called good, a world peopled with man whom He made in his own image and likeness and endowed with the freedom to choose between loving the thing for itself and loving what it signified.

Alberti's treatise described a method of architectural design that the architect's intellectual discipline, talent, and knowledge could use to care for the moral well-being of himself and his fellow citizens. It involved a two-way, reciprocal procedure, one direction moving from the whole, from city to church to column, and the other moving the other way, from column to church to city. This method

---

10. Leon Battista Alberti, *De re aedificatoria*, crit. ed. with en face Italian, trans. Giovanni Orlandi, intro. and notes by Paolo Portoghesi, 2 vols. (Milan: Polifilo, 1966), VII, iii, p. 545; idem, *On the Art of Building in Ten Books*, trans. Joseph Rykwert, Neil Leach, and Robert Tavernor (Cambridge and London: MIT Press, 1988), p. 194. As was characteristic of his circle, Alberti used the word temple for church.

placed the building in a built world consisting of material things that are brought together to produce fully integrated, coherent, proportionate, harmonious, and complete assemblages. The method was as new as the understanding of architecture it served, an understanding that gives equal status to the material that makes buildings visible and the significance that those forms carry, one that seeks to give all the parts and the assemblages their proper places in the world in which the individual, each individual, seeks to fulfill his nature. The column is the principal emblem of this new architecture. It is an architecture in which the column provides the ordering principle for a building's design, the church provides the ordering principle for the city, and the architect provides the design that the skillful craftsman renders in material to produce the buildings and the city.

Brunelleschi had broached this role for the architect. Alberti adumbrated it by extending the principles of perspective to the design of buildings. But the full implications of the use of perspective in the design of buildings required another two generations and the work of two more giants in architecture, Bramante and Michelangelo. The theory and practice of Italian architects from Brunelleschi through Michelangelo made available Christianity's fourth and final contribution to architecture. It consists of defining the architect's role to be that of imitating God's work of creation as he builds in the world. This role made him god-like, a status architects commonly claim today—that is one of the legacies of this contribution—but their claim is solipsistic, not pantheistic. Other religious traditions identify the role of the architect in this world with that of God in the universe, but the Roman pagans, who transmitted the art of architecture to Christianity, did not. As Indra Kagis McEwen has shown in her study of Vitruvius, according to him the role of the architect was to make manifest the deified status of the emperor, but with no similar claim for the architect.[11] In Christianity's Hebraic origins, the architect was subordinate to the person who acted as the intermediary between God and

11. McEwen, *Vitruvius*, passim.

the material structure embodying God's presence among men. Moses followed God's instructions when he directed the craftsmen who built the Ark.[12] Later, when King Solomon responded to God's command to build the Temple, the king apparently provided the design (the Bible is silent about its source), but it explicitly names Hiram of Tyre as his subordinate in executing the design.[13] Even in the papacy of Nicholas V (1447–55), when Alberti was laying the groundwork for moving the role of the architect upward from subordination to equality with the patron, this relationship between builder (Solomon) and architect (Hiram) remained as the type for the relationship between papal patron and architect.[14] The person identified with the New St. Peter's Basilica that Nicholas V planned was Nicholas. But when Julius II (1503–13) took up the project, the architect's elevation was complete, as the closer identification of the present St. Peter's with the architects Bramante and Michelangelo rather than with any of the popes they worked for makes clear. As these ideas that originated in Italian practice and theory become normative throughout Europe over the course of the next several decades, the architect came to be considered the author of buildings that were god-like products imitating God's nature.

The art of this god-like person became established as that of organizing the solids and voids, the buildings and the piazzas, the blocks and the streets, the buildings and the complementary landscape, executed in material within urban and rural areas in imitation of the transcendent moral order that is immanent and visible to man in the world that God made. In designing, the architect no longer works within a precinct's confines. Instead, because during the Crucifixion the Temple's veil was rent, he treats the world as the equivalent of a plenum or

12. "The Lord said to Moses, '... They [the people] shall make an ark of acacia wood; two cubits and a half shall be its length,'" etc.; Ex. 25:1, 10 (RSV).

13. 1 Kings 5:5; 6:14; for Hiram of Tyre, 7:13–14; a fuller, and earlier, role for Hiram (here, Huram-abi) is given in the redaction at 2 Chr. 2:13–14.

14. See my "Biblical Typology in the *Vita Nicolai V* by G. Manetti," *Acta Conventus Neo-Latini Lovaniensis,* Louvain, 1971, ed. by J. IJsewijn and E. Kessler, (Leuven: Leuven University Press, 1973), pp 701–9.

void that has within it a geometric order that his art makes visible. The buildings he places in that world are homomorphic with that plenum's geometric order. That is, they are the solid equivalents of the orderly spatial void in which we act out our lives. We live our lives within a political, civic order that resides in the cities of man, and the architect's buildings and the voids they convert into public places have no other role than serving these cities. If there is no civil order, there is no city, and if no city, no architecture. Contrariwise, if there is no architecture, there is no city, and if no city, no civil order. The civil order is the complement of architecture's order; neither exists without the other; without both of them, order is deficient. In making cities that manifest the reciprocity between solid and void by endowing that void with homogenous geometric order and the buildings that are congruent with it, the architect imitates the beauty of the world God made, and he facilitates the actions of citizens who are cognizant of the moral implications of their acts and who aspire to do the good. This practice in architecture synthesizes ancient ideas about architecture, Augustinian conceptions of beauty and significance, Neoplatonic conceptions of symbolism, Thomistic teachings about natural law, and the less unitary body of political theory developed since its origins in Hellenic Greece.

If we wish to see such an architecture in play, we might look first at Rome (see Figure 2). The Rome we see today is the result of the building program initiated by Pope Nicholas V, a college pal of Alberti to whom Alberti presented his treatise and whom he doubtless advised. The centerpiece of his project called for replacing the Constantinian Basilica at the Tomb of Peter, a project the pope justified with these words:

> [T]he grandeur of buildings, of monuments which are in a sense enduring and appear to testify to the handwork of our Lord, serves to reinforce and confirm that faith of the common people which is based on the assertions of the learned, so that it is then propagated among the living and in the course of time passed on to all those who will

Figure 2. Michelangelo's dome, finished in 1590, and Maderno's façade, from 1614, completed the project begun in 1447 to replace the Constantinian Basilica protecting the Tomb of St. Peter and allow Rome to present indisputable visible evidence of the role the Church aspires to play in the lives of men. *(Photograph by author)*

be enabled to admire these wonderful constructions. This is the only way to uphold and extend the faith so that, preserved and increased in this way, it may be perpetuated with admirable devotion.[15]

Among the "assertions of the learned" stressed in the new building would have been the necessary role of the priesthood in the economy of salvation. The building would make conspicuous the hierarchy of secular and sacred officers culminating in the Pope presiding over the mass at an altar above the Tomb of Peter, the Rock upon whom Christ founded the church.

Nicholas's project languished until 1506 when Julius II, one of the Church's most energetic and authoritarian popes, took it up. The next pope, Leo X, inherited an incomplete project, and we all know the

15. Translation is from James Lawson, "Alberti's Prologue to Practice as a Church Architect: Alberti and Nicholas V on Architecture and the Practice of Religion in the XVth Century," *Albertiana* IV (2001): 46.

melancholic story of the method he used to pay for the project. The sale of indulgences brought to a head a range of issues constituting the Reformation, particularly the role of papal authority in governing the Church, the role of the Church in interpreting revelation and administering the sacraments, and the role of images in Christian rites and ceremonies.

By the time of the Reformation, images had achieved a tremendous potency in presenting doctrine. One of the central images throughout Christian history was that of Rome. Some saw Rome as a type for the Heavenly Jerusalem, while others saw it as the antitype, Babylon. As the popes following Julius II sought to build Rome as a visible embodiment of the New Jerusalem where all could be citizens, some people, particularly those north of the Alps, took it as an ever more potent symbol of Babylon. In 1527, as the Protestants' breach with the authority of Rome was coming to a head, Babylon-Rome was sacked, an event provoked in part by images that represented it as Babylon deserving God's punishment.

During the Reformation, as Eamon Duffy memorably put it, the principal sacrament was iconoclasm. The targets were the images in paint, stone, and glass that were being venerated and the altars where rites and ceremonies of disputed sacrality were conducted. The parts of Europe that were most vehemently iconoclastic and that most readily and energetically fell away from the authority of Rome were the parts that had the weakest connection with the Church's ancient roots. They were the least enmeshed in the panoply of learning, including architectural theory, that constituted the traditional structure of the Church and of the state, and their architectural practices had the weakest link to Greco-Roman traditions. I will return to their side in the dispute in a moment.

During the half-century between Luther's challenge and the conclusion of the Council of Trent in 1563, the Seat of the Head of the Church at St. Peter's was a ruin that could compete with any left from antiquity, an unfortunate but apt representation of the condition of the Church. After Trent had restored to the Church an understanding of its role in the world, the task of rebuilding Jerusalem-Rome was taken up in good earnest. Michelangelo's dome was completed posthumously in 1590, and Maderno's nave and façade twenty-four years later.

The newly completed St. Peter's differed little in its architectural character from what had been in use ever since Brunelleschi and Alberti had invested architecture with its new means of carrying significant and symbolic content. But soon this spare, intellectually based architecture would be considered inadequate to the task the resurgent Church took up. In conducting its Counter Reformation in the seventeenth century, the Church renewed its alliance with architecture as a vehicle for reasserting its claims to authority in religious affairs. Extensive painting and sculpture cycles were pressed into service to supplement the content architecture conveyed in both redecorated older churches and newly built ones. While this figurative art overwhelmed the content of the architectural forms, it did increase the churches' appeal to the eye and thereby present learned doctrine and holy mysteries to laypeople. But during the same period, other new churches kept figurative content at bay while expanding the extra-architectural content. In them, the symbolic content that architecture uniquely made available through its abstract design elements, particularly proportionate relationships and their intertwined geometric configurations, became ever more elaborate, esoteric, and indecipherable, its richest meaning accessible only to a rarified circle of cognoscenti.

The Counter Reformation sought both to reassert its institutional authority in the affairs of people and to make manifest the doctrinal basis of that assertion. Figurative content was one way of doing so, esoteric architectural content was another, and an extension of architecture's control beyond the material solidity of the building into the urban and rural realms was a third. Two projects from the second half of the seventeenth century make this clear, one in Rome, the other in France.

At the Basilica of St. Peter in 1656, Alexander VII had Bernini build the great piazza that extends its reach into Rome and gathers the faithful from throughout the world into the piazza's embracing arms. The arms define an axis along which are aligned the piazza-atrium, narthex, nave, sanctuary with the altar above the Tomb of Peter, and the ancient Cathedra Petri, St. Peter's Episcopal chair encased within Bernini's great reliquary. In the same year he embellished several important entrances into Rome and the ancient Via Triumphalis across the ancient Forum, an important ceremonial route in Roman secular and sacred life, with something never before seen in Mediterranean urbanism, namely, rural components defining urban places. As a legacy of ancient Roman law, cities were under the jurisdiction of urban law and had always been separated by a legal boundary, usually given form in a wall, from their surrounding countryside, which fell under rural law. Alexander breached that separation by using files of trees, an element formerly restricted to rural sites and their facsimiles in enclosed gardens, to demarcate streets within the urban realm. For the first time, plant material was used as a component in the architecture of the public, urban realm. Like the axial reach of Bernini's piazza, these orderly rows of street trees made explicit the extension of Rome's authority and the Church's doctrine beyond any jurisdictional limits imposed by the law of the city of man.

A like claim in the secular realm was not long in coming. In 1661, Louis XIV began restructuring the realm of France using the same architectural means. This involved the destruction of the walls and the construction of boulevards in and around Paris and the projection of tree-lined avenues into and outward from the cities of France. Projecting to the horizon, they were unbounded by territorial limitations. Their origin clearly lay at the royal chateaux, Versailles first among them, where Louis, among whose names was "Gift of God," governed by divine right.

St. Peter's and Versailles stand in stark contrast to Zoser's enclosed precinct at Saqqara, although they are its direct descendents.

Both embody a Christian architecture that supersedes the architecture serving the pre-Christian world. It makes visible in architecture the doctrine that the Grace available through Christianity supersedes the Law given to the Hebrews. That law had been protected within the Ark sheltered in the Temple at Jerusalem inside the Holy of Holies, which was inaccessible except to the highest level of the priesthood and only on special moments in the year's liturgical cycle. All this changed when the Temple's curtain was rent during Christ's crucifixion. With the resurrection the Law, which applied to the chosen people, was replaced by Grace, which is available to all who believe. By the seventeenth century, architecture and the urbanism that corresponds to it had found a means of making visible what St. Paul had enunciated when he said, "For in one spirit we are all baptized into one body—Jews and Greeks, slaves or free—and we are all made to drink of one Spirit" (1 Cor. 12:13).

The Legacy of the Reformation, the Enlightenment, and of Modernism

But of course today, the secular claims the Baroque popes and Divine Right kings made visible in what they built stand in disrepute. We, like Newton but unlike those who lived in earlier centuries than his, understand that the world in which we live is a material realm with continuous, infinitely extensive homogeneous space that can be comprehended within a system of mathematical-geometric order, and that this realm is coterminous with the reach of natural law which is its counterpart in the moral realm.[16] But unlike those who presided over the Church and governed the nations while this understanding of the material and moral universe was being formulated, we accept it as a

16. There is no reason to revise this statement on the basis of Einstein's discoveries and their subsequent development by others. The material world we live in is still homogeneous and the structure of the universe is still a moral one. For the role of a contrary position in the humanities with particular reference to the history of art, see

self-evident truth that we live best when we live in a world dedicated to propositions based on the doctrine that vests authority in majority rule and protects minority rights.[17] Dominant now is the position that the relationship between the individual believer and any institutionalized hierarchy claiming the right to interpret doctrine is non-authoritarian: neither states nor churches within the Judeo-Christian tradition still execute heretics. In the long arc of history, this is a new position that has lead to a vastly different role for architecture as a means of making doctrine visible and a vastly different range of doctrines it makes visible.

In this circumstance the role of the architect as the steward of the art of architecture has changed drastically. Half a millennium ago he emerged from the shadow of the patron to become a person who uses buildings as a means of representing the stand he takes in a moral universe. Since then, architects have played a variety of roles ranging from satraps giving material form to the authority claimed by Divine Right kings to solipsistic celebrities in a sybaritic culture, the former role now as obsolete as the doctrine of Divine Right, the latter now as dominant as our current addiction to stardom. Both roles reveal the full force of the Renaissance formulation that the material forms of buildings embody and convey meaning, that that meaning is identified with the position the architect takes relative to the world, and that that meaning is charged with moral content even if, as in extreme modernism, the content is the negative content of nihilism. That architecture can convey such contradictory content merely reveals the severed link between architecture and authoritative institutions: we no longer look to buildings to tell us about that role authoritative institutions ought to play in our lives. They no longer convey a

---

James Elkins's review of David Summers, *Real Spaces: World Art History and the Rise of Western Modernism, Art Bulletin* LXXXVI (2004): 373–81, esp. 375–77.

17. This epitome of the doctrine is the thread running through Harry V. Jaffe, *A New Birth of Freedom: Abraham Lincoln and the Coming of the Civil War* (Lanham, Boulder, et al.: Rowman & Littlefield, 2000).

common understanding of how we are to live in the world. I will conclude with three illustrations of this point.

The first illustration concerns the fortunes of Protestant architecture; one example will serve to illustrate the larger point.

Those who rejected the authority of Rome built almost nothing for a hundred years. When they did begin building, their chief aim was to avoid looking Catholic and to replace a principally sacramental place of worship with one focused on the word. The first new church building serving the Anglicans was built when the English were having their own troubles with deciding where authority lay in the affairs of the city of man. It was St. Paul's Covent Garden, begun in 1631. Inigo Jones, the founder of English classical architecture, built it as a part of the residential and market development he was designing for the 4th Earl of Bedford behind his London town house. This story later circulated: in telling the architect what he wanted in the development's parish church, the Earl said that he "wou'd not go to any considerable expense; in short, he said, 'I wou'd not have it much better than a barn'. 'Well then', replied Jones, 'you shall have the handsomest barn in England.'"[18]

Likening a church to a barn was not unknown in England during this period. A barn sheltering the produce of the earth is a necessary facility in a domestic household of the sort an English lord governed as a *paterfamilias*. In selecting the model, which was decidedly not Catholic, Jones and his patron were in line with ancient political theory in which the family is the origin of the city. The peace of the family, a peace that derives from the family's just governing by the *paterfamilias,* is essential to the City of God, according to St. Augustine. The dedication of this parish church to St. Paul and the choice of the Tuscan order—the least grand of the canonic five orders, the one closest to the primitive origins of architecture—asserted this ancient theory about the primitive character of the church. Jones's building, Tuscan

18. F. H. W. Sheppard, ed., *Survey of London*, XXXVI: *The Parish of St. Paul Covent Garden* (London: Athlone Press, University of London, 1970), p. 98.

through and through, connects the Church of England with the "purity of the uncorrupted church," the religion of the *domus*, and disconnects it from the Constantinian Church based on the basilica.[19]

St. Paul's Covent Garden was prototypical. It and its successors clarified where authority lay. Like the Church of England and the state that gave it established status, St. Paul's poised the faithful between their rights and duties as parishioners and the rights and duties of the aristocratic and princely class. That is, it put Anglican parishioners within the structure of common law that sought to reconcile the bottom-up customs arising from the day-to-day activities of ordinary people claiming natural rights and the top-down authority exercised by hieratic institutions that natural law justified.

The church building stood hard by Bedford House, the Earl's London residence, and that pair anchored the larger development the Earl built on the old convent grounds, constituting one of the many cells or neighborhoods composing the City of London and its suburbs. The assemblage of London, Protestantism, and the English constitution presents a counterexample to Alexandrine Rome and Louisian France, which belong to architecture as Imhotep had defined it. The legacy of England is one thing; the legacy of the continental Counter Reformation rulers is quite another. Ultimately, after a further three centuries of development, that continental legacy is the modernism that is now hegemonic in architectural theory and practice. Its beginnings are in the excessive claims that top-down authorities in the seventeenth century made in the name of revelation and divine right that were then countered in the eighteenth by excessive claims of reason and the autonomy of conscience, the sorts of claims Jean Jacques Rousseau championed and Edmund Burke condemned. These claims, and their legacy in the political turmoil of the period, gave rise in the

19. Ibid., pp. 98–100. Is St. Paul's a Puritan church or pure Church of England? The question remains open. For the choice of the Tuscan and the place the building in London and in Jones's oeuvre, see John Summerson, *Inigo Jones* (Harmondsworth: Penguin, 1966), pp. 83–96.

nineteenth century to a secularism and romanticism that were linked to an idealism that justified, in the twentieth century, severing all connections with traditional practices in architecture and the traditional alliances between philosophy, learning, and theories concerning the practice of architecture. This modernism provides my second illustration.

Modernism has achieved what it set out to accomplish, namely, to destroy tradition as the basis for its building practices. But the modernists, despite their success in wrecking tradition, embrace the traditional belief that architecture has content, that the content is more than merely the beauty of *venustas* (or the demonstration of novelty), that architecture's beauty also has a moral content, and that that moral content can be void of religious content. That is, they seek to do what traditional architecture has been able to do ever since Alberti taught us that the architect's greatest value lies in his ability to make the moral order of the world visible, which is one of Christianity's contributions to architecture. The modernists' hundred-year failure to do so on their terms reveals the futility of a purely secular basis for the enterprise.

Alberti explained that, because the architecture could carry the building's symbolic meaning, it did not need images in the form of paintings, sculpture, and stained glass, embellishments such as paint or gilding, or other things that would distract the worshipper from the holy mysteries vouchsafed to the Church. The church building's principal focus would be a single altar, and that altar would be used sparingly, lest overuse vitiate the potency of the sacrifice of the mass. This was a spare, pietistic approach to architecture that hardly survived the Counter Reformation within the Catholic Church, although it became, and remains, the basis for much Protestant architecture. Eventually the modernists found it amenable to architectural theories that bear only the most debased connection with the religious doctrines that invested those forms with theological substance. The architectural practice linked to those theories of architecture can be illustrated by the so-called "God Box" that Mies van der Rohe built at the Illinois Institute of Technology in Chicago in 1952 and any number of other larger, grander examples, including many Christian churches designed by modernists of every religious stripe (see Figure 3).

Mies's little building, and its relatives everywhere, raise the question, Why would modernism even attempt to build a special box for God when in its core modernism finds no role for God in its world? To be sure, there are modernist architects who design churches with anti-traditional, modernist forms, but those efforts contradict the central quest of modernism, which rejects revelation as a source of authority. This rejection calls to mind the definition of Christianity I gave at the outset, that it contains "a revelation of Himself, which all to whom it has been adequately presented are bound under pain of eternal loss to accept." That is a harsh doctrine for those who reject revelation, but perhaps no less harsh than its antidote is powerful, namely, the power of the Christian aesthetic and the theory it entails. Unfortunately, in the name of architecture, modernists have impoverished that power by seeking and propagating an architecture that is antithetical to the fundamental basis of architecture but that nonetheless claims to be architecture and to be capable of producing church buildings that play the role Alberti had explicated.

The two examples, one from the seventeenth century, the other from the twentieth, illustrate two different ways to exercise authority and to build in this world. The Earl of Bedford's residential development pushes upward from the bottom, and Mies's modernism seeks to impose order from on high. The genius of the American Founders was to put into play a politics encompassing these two extremes. The top-down authority seeks to bring citizens together to achieve a common good, and individuals exercising their natural right to pursue their own happiness provide a bottom-up counterbalance. To put it in architectural and urban terms, the one seeks to build houses that, people hope, accumulate into cities, while the other sets out to build cities that hold houses. The balance between bottom-up liberty and

Figure 3. The chapel Ludwig Mies van der Rohe designed for the campus at the Illinois Institute of Technology in Chicago in 1950 has managed to void architecture of all traditional content. *(Photograph by author)*

top-down authority produces the never-ending dialectic giving body to the good, the true, and the beautiful actions of the authoritative institutions that discipline the ever-changing circumstances of this life.

This politics and the architecture that serves it provide my third illustration, which exists as a legacy of Christianity. Our first parents were given free reign in the Garden so long as they did not eat of the forbidden fruit. The Christian enjoys his freedom within the Law of Christ. In our polity the interplay is clearly presented in the lintel inscription of the Palmyra County Courthouse in Virginia from 1836: "The MAXIM held sacred by all free people: OBEY THE LAW."

Within the traditions of this country, the mature embodiment of that political doctrine in urban form is in the paradigmatic form of the American polity. This paradigm first took form in Williamsburg. Its foundation in 1699 predates that of the republic, but it nonetheless informs the republic's early architecture just as the political experience of the colonies provided experience essential for forming the new union of states (see Figure 4).

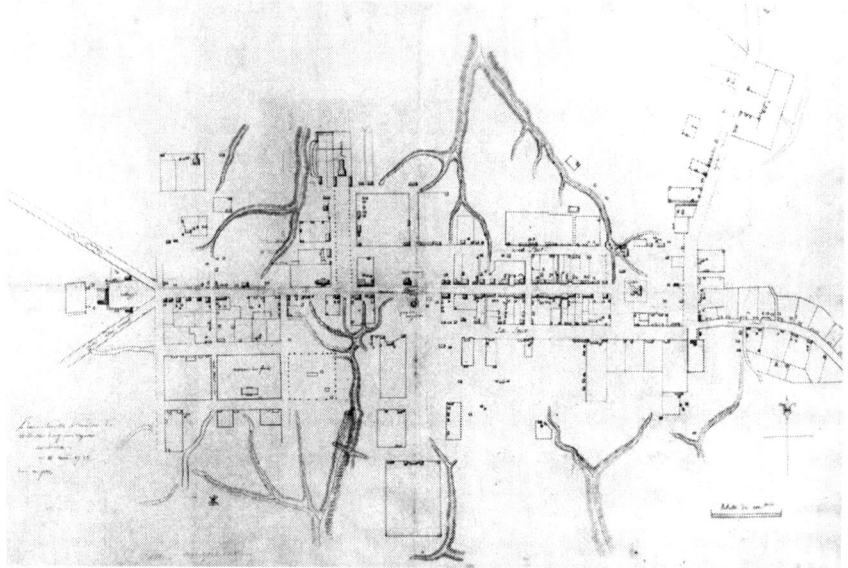

Figure 4. Williamsburg, Virginia, shown here in a 1782 map, was built following the 1699 plan of Governor Nicholson, which planted a city within its complementary rural countryside, with the axial relationships that organized the streets, open areas, and house plots revealing the independence and interdependence of the various governing civil and religious institutions. *(Photograph courtesy of Special Collections Research Center, Swem Library, College of William and Mary)*

At Williamsburg, set onto the land and making way for the land's deformities, is a grid defining the streets and alleys between the private parcels forming the municipality of Williamsburg. This town is focused on the market square holding a courthouse for adjudicating local affairs and a powder magazine and muster room for the militia. Overlaid on this grid is the larger geometry holding the institutions whose authority reaches beyond the town to the colony as a whole. Along the ridgeline, a street devoted to commerce forms an axis running through the central square and connecting the State House and the College, which had been built before the town was platted. On that axis is another pre-existing building, the Bruton Parish Church.

At the churchyard the axis is joined by the wide greensward running up to the Governor's Mansion in one direction and opening out to the cultivated rural landscape in the other.

Here is the kernel of the American city. Enlarged, it became the Federal District of Washington. Reduced, it produced the innumerable county courthouse towns spread across the great grid American of the American frontier. Here is the urban embodiment of the intersection of the bottom-up authority of the majority and the top-down authority entrusted to the Constitution.

That Constitution enjoins the top-down authority from making any "law respecting an establishment of religion, or prohibiting the free exercise thereof." It is notable that the Bruton Parish Church sits beside the intersection of the axes of secular power, that of the people in the capitol and the governor in his palace. It is not at the intersection of the axes, and certainly not at the end of an axis. It is nestled within the structure of secular government, and in the new polity it would be disestablished and protected from that secular authority by a government injunction. How the people will use their freedom to exercise their religion is up to them.

The disestablishment of religious institutions and the secularization of governmental authority are two cardinal tenets of the modern world. When these tenets are accompanied by a balance between the natural law, which seeks the common good, and natural right, which sanctions the individual's pursuit of his own happiness, they can establish a peaceful city of man in which the City of God can flourish. In this situation, architecture can represent the comity between church and state and between the individual and the polity, and it can facilitate the aspirations of people of good will as they pursue their individual ends. The early Republic produced numerous examples of such a material embodiment of the nation's ideals, flawed as those ideas were in the actual legal and social structure in which they were played out. The New England town, Thomas Jefferson's "academical village" at the University of Virginia, the city of Savanna, Georgia, and the Midwestern courthouse town provide small-scale examples of physical places superior to the legal, economic, and social justice prevailing in them. But more recently, as our expectations about the justice available to all our citizens has risen, the quality of our cities, towns, and rural countryside has declined.

That decline points to the maxim that politics is more important than architecture. The regime, or the authoritative institutional structure and the way people live together under law, controls the framework within which they pursue the art of architecture. Unfortunately, we have long been in headlong pursuit of individualistic rather than communitarian ends. In this circumstance, those who are responsible for architecture consider themselves independent of any authority that might dictate how architecture is to be brought to the service of institutions that seek the common good, whether those institutions be secular or sacred. Instead of living within a long-standing and ever-modernizing tradition, we have modernism, which considers tradition antithetical to its ends, which is nihilistic when it is not merely secular, and which seeks a city of man void of the City of God.

The Roman Catholic Church, as we have seen, has had a deep and sustained alliance with architecture. But neither its pronouncements nor its patronage indicate that it is aware of the extent to which current theories and fashions in architecture are antithetical to the Church's doctrine and purposes. Not that other Christians have done any better. Christians across the board tend to disregard the capacity of the visible properties of buildings to give form to their doctrines. Among non-Catholics this negligence is perhaps the legacy of the Reformation, which rejected the image and placed primary value on the Word. Among Catholics, it is perhaps yet another example of the unresolved conflict between the Church's doctrines and the forces of modernity. In both cases, the result is that those who build churches tend to accept as architecture that which architects say is architecture. Newly built churches will continue to illustrate current architectural theories rooted in secularism so long as churches fail to provide a doctrinal framework that can call forth an architecture worthy of the church's mission.

This situation in architecture resembles the one John Paul II outlined for philosophy in the encyclical *Faith and Reason.* In that document he condemns several current positions in philosophy, each of which plays a formative role in current architectural theory and practice. The Holy Father sees the potential of a renewed role for philosophy in serving the faith. We might hope for a similar renewal of the architecture serving faith.

The result will not be the kind of overreaching that is visible in Counter Reformation practice. Instead, I would expect a pluralism similar to that found in religious practices, a pluralism that ushers forth from the First Amendment's protection of religion from the intrusions of secular authority. Because architecture inevitably and necessarily serves and elucidates the doctrinal basis for those practices, we should reasonably expect to see a variety of forms for buildings serving religion. But we ought to expect that buildings serving religions such as the Catholic Church—which nourish the faith by interpreting doctrine, bringing reason to that task, and accumulating those interpretations into a body of traditional knowledge—would seek an architecture that embodies and makes visible this magisterium. Nothing less would seem to answer to the call that the architect is to answer, namely, to make visible in architectural form the goodness, truth, and beauty that reside at the very heart of the Church, the body of Christ, qualities that originate in God and that form the very foundation of our polity and culture, whether or not we choose to acknowledge that this is so.

three

Ralph McInerny

LITERATURE AND GEORGES BERNANOS

Only by the recovery of the mystery of the human person, and the sense of the profundity of freedom and human destiny, can the trivialization of human existence be overcome.

There are three kinds of Catholic writer. There are authors who are Catholic and whose novels turn on the lore of the faith (Waugh, Greene, J. F. Powers). There are non-Catholic authors whose novels deal with Catholics in a profoundly convincing way (pre-eminently Willa Cather in *Death Comes for the Archbishop* and *Shadows on the Rock*). And then there are Dante and Georges Bernanos.

In the dedicatory letter to Can Grande della Scala, Dante applies to his great poem techniques that had been developed for the interpretation of Sacred Scripture. The literal meaning of the Comedy is the state of souls after death. Its allegorical meaning is the way in which human beings, by the exercise of their free will, justly determine their eternal state of punishment or reward. In Dante—and the same is true of Georges Bernanos—characters are seen in the light of the ultimate stakes of life, of damnation or salvation, and of good and evil read in the light of those.

It may seem that this does not distinguish Dante and Bernanos from Catholic writers in the other senses I have given. Indeed, if Flannery O'Connor is right, it may not seem to distinguish them even from non-Catholic writers. She said that all literature, as in *all,* is anagogical; that is, takes its meaning from the transcendent reference of human actions. So let me dwell a bit on what such a writer as Bernanos has in common with any serious writer as well as with other Catholic writers before I return to what sets him, and Dante, off.

C. S. Lewis, in *Experiment in Criticism,* asked himself how we distinguish literature from other things we like to read but are somewhat diffident about, say, an Elmore Leonard western or an Agatha Christie. How does the professor of literature set his professional interests off from the kind of thing he and everybody else enjoy reading but which he would hesitate to call literature? What is literature? Lewis began with this rule of thumb: Literature is anything we would read again. He then goes on to discuss what brings us back to a book, sometimes again and again.

One of the things he is out to do is suggest a spectrum along which we can locate a great variety of imaginative works. He is by no means adopting a leveling view of the kind that has become depressingly familiar, the sort of view Harold Bloom lamented in *The Western Canon* and John Carey has, alas, recently adopted in *What Good Is Art?* The same John Carey who wrote the magnificent *The Intellectuals and the Masses.*

So why is re-reading a good starting point? You may know the story of the candidate for the French Academy who was lobbying the Immortals for their votes and obsequiously approached one particularly Olympian figure, kissed his foot and all the rest, and then asked timidly,

"Have you read me?" The great man's brows went up. *"Je ne lis pas. Je re-lis."* What do we reread for? It may be for many things—the setting, the plot, the characters, the language, the humor, and any number of these in combination. But probably what is most prominent in our ranking of imaginative works is conveyed by the voice of the author. Think of picking up anything of Joseph Conrad's again; one enters once more into an utterly distinctive world, and what the voice conveys is a vision of the meaning of life, of the significance of action. The more profound an insight an author gives into the mystery of human action, the higher we would rank him.

Aristotle tells us that poetry—imaginative writing—is precisely an imitation of human action. We follow the deeds of imaginary characters as they confront a problem, a dilemma, a crossroads. What will they do, how will they act? Will they, like Lord Jim, betray the trust of those confided to them, and what then? The particular imagined act is presented against an interpretative background that gives it the meaning it has, a meaning that transcends particularity and determines the character of the agent. I think that this is what Flannery O'Connor meant when she said that all literature is anagogical.

One could go on about this, but that is not my task today. Imagine that I had established to your satisfaction that it is for just this transcendent meaning of the action displayed that we go to fiction. Imagine that I had established that gradations of this meaning are to be found in the things that we would read again. The things that we would read but once may simply divert and please, but they are somewhat like Kleenex—one use and out.

But other things are reread and ranked, and some we would place at the top of the scale.

If this is true of all literature, what does Catholic literature add to it? I suppose we could invoke St. Thomas's distinction between natural and supernatural beatitude. Any work of literature will assess action, more or less explicitly, in terms of what is truly fulfilling of what we are. The virtues and vices displayed can be read in terms of our natural end.

If this is so, Catholic literature will up the ante by invoking the supernatural end of human life. The same kind of deeds any writer deals with take on a valence that refers them beyond this life, to salvation or damnation. But then how can we distinguish among Catholic writers, as I did at the outset?

Willa Cather's archbishop as well as her Monseigneur Laval and Graham Greene's Major Scobie are all seen in the light of their ultimate salvation or damnation. So how do Dante and Georges Bernanos differ from other Catholic writers? It is a matter of degree, of intensity, of seeing the story overtly in terms of the supernatural stakes of action. Salvation or damnation are not merely implicit in the story; they are the story.

Georges Bernanos [1888–1948] was thirty-eight years old when his first novel, *Under the Sun of Satan,* was published in 1926. It is a remarkable novel whose power is easily felt by the English reader in the Harry Lorin Binsse translation that appeared in 1949. (An earlier, less effective translation had appeared in 1940.) The prologue is a chilling portrait of evil: The Story of Mouchette.

Mouchette is a sixteen-year-old girl who, when the story opens, is pregnant by a womanizing marquis, a fact she denies to her father, who nonetheless confronts the marquis and is laughed out of the room. That night, Mouchette sneaks out and visits the marquis, anxious to assure him that she did not tell her father. The marquis is puzzled by this. Subtly, subtly, Bernanos opens before us a girl who has chosen to be evil, not simply to act wrongly. She lies, not to save herself or the marquis or her parents, but in order to lie. The emotional mutations of this scene with the marquis move plausibly and inexorably to Mouchette's shooting the marquis.

The next set scene presents Mouchette, now three months pregnant, in a doctor's waiting room. We learn that she is now having an affair with the doctor, whom she tries to convince that he is the father of her child. He dismisses this, she doesn't press it, and the scene becomes a cat and mouse game, in which the girl toys with a frantic, frightened, middle-aged man whose wife is upstairs.

Later, Bernanos wrote *La Nouvelle Histoire de Mouchette*. The Mouchette of the novel is sixteen; the Mouchette of the later novella is fourteen. Is she merely an earlier version of the former? She cannot be, because the later novella ends with her suicide. It wasn't simply that Bernanos liked the name; he seems to have paired the two girls in terms of damnation and salvation. The *New Story of Mouchette* is noteworthy for the fact that the supernatural remains implicit, but when the girl drowns herself there is something paradoxically salvific, even baptismal, in her action.

No summary can possibly convey the skill with which Bernanos creates a portrait of a young girl's gratuitous evil in the novel. It is a prologue, but a prologue to what? To a portrait of sanctity, of a young country bumpkin priest modeled on the Curé d'Ars.

Moral failure is easier to imagine and to portray than virtue or heroism. Still, many artists have given us convincing, moving, ennobling portraits of heroism. But moral failure is not evil, nor is heroism sanctity. Georges Bernanos, from the outset of his literary career, had an almost unique ability to provide his reader with an unforgettable sense of the stakes of life: good or evil, heaven or hell, God or Satan.

This first novel was not a fluke, a unique achievement. *Imposture* (1928), *Joy* (1929) and *Diary of a Country Priest* (1936) continue Bernanos's amazing performance. Hoping to make some money, he tried to write a murder mystery *(A Crime),* but he could not confine himself to the stylization of moral fault, as the genre may seem to require; inevitably, as it seems, the book was transformed into something far more, something profound, something that tapped the very well-springs of human action. A failed mystery novel became a work of art.

Who was this man who in his late thirties commenced a literary career of such depth? After four years of service in World War I, Georges Bernanos married and sold insurance in the provinces. Born in Paris, educated by Jesuits he loathed, far right, a member of Action Française and indeed a lifetime royalist, he might have seemed an enthusiastic and doctrinaire young man. His war experience and then marriage tilted him in the direction of middle-class respectability. Wife, family, selling insurance—against that background, the novels surprise, even astound.

The truth is that from boyhood, Georges Bernanos's faith permeated his view of life. He was anti-democratic because he felt that modern political life trivialized the human agent, the free, intelligent person whose deeds and decisions in this life are decisive for eternity. His break with Action Française, his subsequent rejection of the Franco cause in Spain *(The Great Cemeteries under the Moon),* display a man who judged politics from a religious point of view, not vice versa.

Looked upon simply as fiction, Bernanos's work can be seen as a corrective to the banality of much modern fiction. But it is a corrective taken in the name of the importance of the subject of fiction, namely, the responsible human agent with an eternal destiny.

In 1934, aged forty-six, after suffering a motorcycle accident that left him lame, Bernanos moved with his family to Majorca in an effort to keep down expenses, and four years later he moved to South America, Paraguay briefly, then Brazil. Thus it was from exile that this quintessential Frenchman, whose love of his country survived his disgust with and criticism of its moral and political tone, wrote the great non-fiction polemics which, added to his fiction, make him one of the greatest of French authors.

The Spanish Civil War presented many with a crossroads. Doctrinaire leftists and fellow travelers supported the Republic unquestioningly, a certain kind of Catholic blindly supported Franco. There were noble exceptions among French—and American—Catholics, and none more noble than Georges Bernanos. (It is interesting to compare his eventual judgment of a pox on both your houses with that of Simone Weil.) Living in Majorca, Bernanos had close-up experience of what was at issue. The late Thirties, and then the Second World War, swept Bernanos into a new role as a polemicist. Combative, prophetic, angry, Bernanos spoke from the heart to his countrymen throughout the war and the agony of occupation.

Summoned by General De Gaulle, he returned to France in 1945, but he remained unclubbable. The Fourth Republic became the new target of his criticism. He was furious when it was proposed that he put himself forward for the French Academy. He avoided being honored by a society he considered corrupt, even after the crucible of its defeat and occupation. On three separate occasions he refused the Legion of Honor.

Such a late work as *France against the Robots,* treating the mechanization of human life, can be read today for its perceptiveness. "A world dominated by power is an abominable world, but a world dominated by number is ignoble." We, in a society governed by polls, where self-knowledge and self-appraisal are sought through surveys and questionnaires, are painfully aware of the quantification and false-objectification of human existence. Bernanos did not look to politics, now become the manipulation of citizens, for the remedy of modern ills. Only by the recovery of the mystery of the human person, and the sense of the profundity of freedom and human destiny, can the trivialization of human existence be overcome. Is there any wonder that Pope John Paul II came back again and again to the nature of the human person?

It would be interesting to contrast Bernanos and Graham Greene, who after such a novel as *The Labyrinthine Ways,* in which the reluctant martyr is pitted against the Jefe, the political, after *Brighton Rock, The Heart of the Matter, The End of the Affair,* turns in *The Honorary Consul* and later novels to a political interpretation of action. This is a turn Bernanos could never have taken.

Bernanos foresaw what would happen when humans began to see themselves as robots, as machines responsive to extrinsic causes, their actions mere reactions. Nowadays even bishops speak of the misbehavior of the clergy, for example, as corrigible by means of counseling, therapy, external causes. The concept of sin, of moral responsibility, has been weakened.

Shortly before he died, in 1948, in a letter to an old friend, Bernanos closed with a remark that sums up his vision of life. "May you feel the sweet presence of Jesus Christ who makes into one reality sorrow and joy, life and death." Bernanos was incapable of an unctuous remark or of pietism. He speaks here—he could not speak otherwise—out of the abundance of his heart. His novels give us Catholic fiction, not as an interesting sub-genre, but as the only truly serious viewpoint from which the mystery of human existence can be imaginatively grasped.

Bernanos's favorite character is a priest or religious. The father of six, unmistakably a layman, not a little anticlerical, there was much of the spoiled priest about Bernanos. There is a photograph of him as a young boy wearing a soutane, looking very sacerdotal. He supported his family precariously by his writing, but he had a view of his task that set him apart from other authors. He both did and did not want to be considered one of them. Like Flannery O'Connor, he unabashedly saw his writing as his vocation, and in the full sense of that term. In *A Diary of a Country Priest* he writes in the first person, as the young curé whose story he tells. In all his fiction there is a pastoral concern for his characters as he views what they are doing in the light of their ultimate destiny. We are not surprised to learn that Dostoievski was a favorite of his. Some stories, even as they depict action in the most ordinary and familiar settings, take us immediately beneath the skin of the present to the ultimate assessment.

Consider the difference between the priests of Bernanos and those of that excellent writer J. F. Powers. Powers wrote only a handful of stories that do not have a priest as their main character. From *The Prince of Darkness and Other Stories,* through *Morte d'Urban* to *Wheat that Springeth Green,* the priest is in the forefront. As often as not, the action turns on a point of consummate triviality—the pastor's automobile; whether a pastor can avoid being drawn into a nightly card game with his housekeeper; whether a priest who helped out in a parish on a weekend and left in the wrong trousers can return them without calling attention to his gaucherie; a priest's meeting with the bishop about a new appointment—with no overt dwelling on the function of a priest. The reader is expected to provide that for himself and read the stories accordingly. Not so with Bernanos.

The young priest whose diary we read is a portrait of sanctity. He is awkward, a hobbledehoy, as Trollope would say, inept, a subject of amusement for his fellow priests and of contempt by his upscale parishioners. In his dealings with himself and with others, there is always in play the realization that what we do concerns the state of our soul. How this is done without cloying religiosity is one of the great mysteries of Bernanos's genius. His novels can make those of even the greatest of Catholic novelists seem relatively superficial. With him, every moment may be the last, decisive one. "Thou fool, this very night thy soul may be required of thee." All goals less than salvation or its opposite are viewed in their light. In his pastoral work, the young curé deals with a young girl whose mother's treatment of her has caused her to think like Milton's Satan, "Evil be thou my good." In his interview with the haughty countess, the girl's mother, the curé pierces through her façade to see that she has spent her life seething with resentment over the loss of a son. In a powerfully plausible scene, he enables her to see the state of her soul. His correspondence with and then visit to a defrocked classmate has a poignancy that in lesser hands would have been either comic or banal. With Bernanos, it is tragic, but suffused with the mercy of charity. The woman with whom the classmate is living is one of the most touching figures in twentieth-century French literature. The novel, which takes place over the course of a year, ends with the death by cancer of the young curé.

Albert Beguin has pointed out that the two poles of Bernanos's imagination are childhood and death. Bernanos once said that the reader for whom he wrote is the boy he had been. Childhood is a time not so much of innocence as of ignorance of evil, that period before one is plunged into the circumstances and decisions which will decide his ultimate destiny. Death, as the grim boundary between time and eternity, the moment when one is frozen into the self he has constructed, haunts the stories. And never more so than in *Dialogue of the Carmelites*.

Set in a Parisian Carmelite Convent in the bloody path of the French Revolution, this play, screenplay actually, moves from opening scenes in which the peace and tranquility of the conventual contemplative life is conveyed through the progressive trepidations of revolutionary politics, the invasion of the convent, to the eventual martyrdom of the sisters. This work, Bernanos's last—he had hoped to write a life of Jesus, but death intervened—has a complicated provenance. The German writer Getrude von le Fort had written a novel that the French Dominican Bruckberger altered into a film script set at the time of the French Revolution. Bruckberger appealed to Bernanos to write dialogue for it, hence the title of the eventual work. Despite its origins, this is unmistakably Bernanos's own work. A young Carmelite of aristocratic origins is presented before her entry into the convent as subject to fear, wanting in fortitude, attractively weak. Her vocation is perhaps a bit of a refuge in her own mind, and yet by entering the convent she has unwittingly placed herself in what will become a place of maximum danger to her very life. She wavers, she weakens, she flees, but in the end, with her community, she mounts the scaffold, her fear overcome at last. The play provides the most overt opposition we have in Bernanos of the political and the religious.

No one could survive on an exclusive diet of Bernanos. Perhaps, as with Dante, he provides an ultimate criterion of true greatness from which other writers decline. Most of us need those other writers as well, not simply to appreciate the contrast, but because the intensity of interpretation is so overwhelming. "The human mind cannot bear very much reality," as Eliot said. The point of invoking C. S. Lewis earlier was precisely to suggest that there is a scale, a spectrum, on which imaginative works are located at various points. And in many cases, at different points over our lifetime. Perhaps what Lewis was countering was the tendency to think that we should read only works that are the most objectively re-readable, a tendency that leaves us apologetic and shamefaced when we are discovered reading P. G. Wodehouse or even *Huckleberry Finn*. But the best should not be the enemy of the good and more than good, and there are times when what is readable only once is just what we need.

It is easy to write bad Catholic fiction, but then it is easy to write bad fiction *tout court.* Well, maybe not easy, but what usually happens. It is tempting to write psychological novels that reduce actions to mechanical antecedents; it is tempting to write from some fleeting political or ideological point of view. And it is tempting to use Catholicism as an exotic ingredient in an otherwise hackneyed story. Or worse, to preach. It is that latter tendency that explains why so many Catholic novelists have not wanted to be called Catholic novelists. Consider the case of Flannery O'Connor. As far as I know, Catholic things appear overtly in few of her stories, notably in "Temples of the Holy Ghost." But it is not only her letters that justify our thinking of her as a Catholic novelist.

And she was not above a little preaching in her letters. Like Bernanos, she could be irritated by official, often clerical, requirements of fiction. But she never displayed the bombast and fury of Bernanos when he went after those he called imbeciles. He quarreled with Paul Claudel, he quarreled with Jacques Maritain. He was quintessentially unclubbable. Beguin tells of a night-time automobile trip with Bernanos in which the writer ranted and raved for hours. Then silence. And then the gentle remark that of course he too was an imbecile.

Not everyone's cup of tea. And even if he is, teatime is not always. I began by likening Bernanos and Dante. Let me end with an important common note between the two men, their devotion to the Blessed Virgin. In Canto 33 of the Paradiso, St. Bernard praises Mary as no other woman could ever have been praised. In a passage put in the mouth of an older priest who is encouraging the young curé, Bernanos speaks of the Blessed Virgin as a child. But if children are ignorant of evil, she is innocent of it. In a memorable phrase, Mary is said to be "younger than sin." Immaculately conceived, unstained by Original Sin—our tainted nature's solitary boast—how must we seem to her in our weaknesses and sin? No wonder we elicit her mercy. Bernanos seems unwittingly to be conveying his attitude toward his characters. John Updike said of Salinger that he loved his characters more than God could. Few authors have, like Bernanos, tried to love their characters as much as God does.

four

⁓

Peter John Cameron, O.P.

THEATER AND THE EVANGELIZATION

OF CULTURE

The Christian drama happens at the level of the individual, at the level of the person, and the rest derives from it.

Monsignor Luigi Giussani

Twenty-four-hour television on one thousand and thirty-four dif-ferent channels; a dozen new movies every month offered by way of the local cineplex, on video cassette, DVD, pay-per-view, or via the Internet; Broadway tickets that cost one hundred dollars or more yet still are sometimes impossible to get; and so it goes. Given the pre-dominance of all these factors, why has the art known as *theater* not gone out of existence? What is it about the theater—so integral to hu-man experience—that keeps it from becoming extinct?

Looking at what is uniquely distinctive about the theater, I intend in this essay to propose theater as an invaluable instrument of the re-evangelization of culture.

The Human Drama

What is it about the human heart that theater manages to reach in such an indispensable and indefatigable way? According to our late Holy Father Pope John Paul II, "the basic human drama is the failure to perceive the meaning of life, to live without a meaning." In other words, for so many the sense of *destiny* has not been awakened in them. One main reason why the human being lives bereft of the meaning of life is because he has nothing to inspire him to search the depths of his self so as to discover the truth of his human "I." The person who does confront the evidence of his own existence comes face to face with three key truths about the human "I": first, I didn't make myself; second, I have desires that I did not give myself and that I cannot remove, desires that are infinite in their scope; and third, I live with the expectation that I will be happy—the certainty that I have been promised meaning and fulfillment in my life.

This awareness of the fundamental facts of my existence provokes three correlative and urgent questions in my soul:

1. If I did not make myself, then who made me? I say "who" because my awakened self-awareness summons up in me a certainty that my Maker is in some way like me and that I am in relationship with my Maker; that is, my Maker had a reason for making me.

2. My desires give me evidence that there is something about me which is infinite, and so I am led to ask: Is there some One who is infinite who gave me these desires and who wills to satisfy these otherwise insatiable desires?

3. Who can meet my expectations for happiness? Every attempt on my part falls short and leaves me disappointed. If I am sure that I have been promised fulfillment, who put that promise in me in the first place? I am convinced that the One who made that promise alone can make it come true.

These three questions combine to form the one great and Ultimate Question, namely, What is the meaning of life? At the point that this question is posed, reason begins to operate at its optimal level. The "I," animated, aware, and perhaps even anguished, shares in the Passion of the dying Christ on the Cross who cries out: "I thirst!" The human "I" itself is thirst . . . thirsting to know its meaning, its mission, its purpose, its destiny. The zenith of reason's power is reason's awareness of its own limitations. Yet, while reason cannot provide an adequate answer to the ultimate question that it raises, reason does arrive at the perception of a Mystery beyond itself . . . a Mystery that is a Presence that corresponds to the most urgent longings of the human heart.

This surmising, this judgment on the part of reason, is an *act of imagination that calls out for imagination.* And this is where theater comes in. In the fifth volume of his work entitled *Theo-drama,* Hans Urs von Balthasar wrote:

> The task of the stage is to make the drama of existence explicit so that we may view it. . . . Where existence is directly interpreted as theatre, the "I" must be understood as the role. . . . It continually delivers man from the sense of being trapped and from the temptation to regard existence as something closed in upon itself. Through the theatre, man acquires the habit of looking for meaning at a higher and less obvious level. . . . Theatre's intrinsic function [is] to be a place where man can look in a mirror in order to recollect himself and remember who he is. . . . In the theatre man attempts a kind of transcendence, endeavoring both to observe and to judge his own truth, in virtue of a transformation . . . by which he tries to gain clarity about himself. . . . Theatre is no sinful illusion but the necessity of, and pleasure in, seeing oneself portrayed by another; in this "mask" the "person" both loses and finds himself.[1]

So we can say that the human heart craves the theater because the human heart lives waiting for something that will reveal the meaning

---

1. Hans Urs von Balthasar, *Theo-drama: Theological Dramatic Theory: The Last Act,* trans. Graham Harrison (San Francisco: Ignatius Press, 1998), Vol. V, pp. 17, 173, 20, 86, 12, 122.

of being human. For some reason, something deeply rooted in the human soul compels it to look to the "imitation of human beings in action"[2]—which is how Aristotle defines tragic drama in the *Poetics*—in order to discover a clue about its destiny. Theater in the service of the New Evangelization seeks to engage reason on this level.

Of course, the great challenge to theater committed to bringing light to souls is how to stir people out of their anesthetized lives, how to motivate people to break through the crust they have allowed to form over their day-to-day existence. To do this, theater must penetrate to the precise core of what people care about. It must respond to a lived question. It must attract and compel on the deepest level of meaning. It must interact with others at the point in which life begins to spark and flame. Otherwise, theater remains at best an irrelevant distraction.

According to the great novelist and playwright Thornton Wilder, the author of the beautiful American classic play *Our Town,* the best strategy for creating compelling theater is to show original sin. Wilder wrote:

> Gazing deeply into the problem of mankind's agonized straining under the problem of original sin [one should place] on the stage not a discussion of original sin but a living, suffering example of original sin. That's what the theater's for. That's what the theater is. It has a far more glorious function than the lecture hall and the discussion forum: it is where you show the human situation.[3]

Because what is original sin? Original sin is the claim that we can identify the total meaning of life with something that we can comprehend and control, something we can measure, manage, and manipulate. Original sin attempts to identify God with some idol that is of our own choosing. The impulse of original sin is to attempt to identify the answer to the ultimate question of life with a particular aspect of our self.

---

2. Aristotle, *The Poetics,* trans. Ingram Bywater *(New York: Random House, 1941).*

3. Gilbert A. Harrison, *The Enthusiast: A Life of Thornton Wilder* (New Haven & New York: Ticknor & Fields, 1983), p. 313.

Thornton Wilder insists that a "discussion" of original sin will not suffice; what is needed is a dramatic *experience* of original sin. "Showing" the human situation in turn offers an opportunity for the person to perfect the human situation.

Theater's Connection with Culture

In efforts aimed at advancing in perfection, the integral link between culture and theater becomes clear. *Gaudium et Spes* tells us that the human person "can achieve true and full humanity only by means of culture."[4] But what is the key to a Gospel understanding of "culture"? One theologian who has dedicated his long priestly ministry to articulating and nurturing the Church's notion of culture is Monsignor Luigi Giussani. Monsignor Giussani is the founder of the ecclesial movement Communion and Liberation. An outstanding hallmark of the charism of Communion and Liberation is its devotion to culture. Giussani writes:

> We define culture as the critical, systematic development of an experience. An experience is an event that opens us to the totality of reality: experience always implies a comparison between what one feels and what one believes to be the ultimate ideal or meaning. Culture works to unfold this implication of wholeness and totality which is part of every human experience.[5]

Elsewhere he says, "Culture is that from which man draws . . . inspiration for his way of behaving . . . in the affirmation of the ultimate aim of what he does, that is to say, his destiny."[6]

4. Vatican Council II. *Gaudium et Spes*, in *Vatican Council II, The Basic Edition: Constitutions, Decrees, Declarations,* ed. Austin Flannery, O.P. (Northport, NY: Costello Publishing Company, Inc., 1996), II. 53.

5. Luigi Giussani, *Risk of Education*, trans. Rossanna M. G. Frongia (New York: Crossroads Publishing Company, 2001), p. 133.

6. Luigi Giussani, *The Exercises of the Fraternity of Communion and Liberation* (Rimini: Fraternita de comunione e liberatione, 1998), p. 14.

Theater is an event in which experience thrives, for, as Giussani writes, "True experience throws us into the rhythms of the real, drawing us irresistibly toward our union with the ultimate aspect of things and their true definitive meaning."[7] Authentic theater yearns for nothing less. One of the most influential modern theorists of theater whose ideas revolutionized theater—ideas that continue to hold sway in the theater to this day—was the French actor and playwright Antonin Artaud. Although Artaud had little use for faith or religion, he nevertheless professed:

> The true purpose of theatre . . . is to express life in its immense, universal aspect, and from that life to extract images in which we find pleasure in discovering ourselves. . . . When we speak the word "life", it must be understood we are not referring to life as we know it from its surface of fact, but to that fragile, fluctuating center which forms never reach. . . . [The object of theatre is] to express objectively certain secret truths, to bring into the light of day by means of active gestures certain aspects of truth that have been buried under forms in their encounters with Becoming. . . . The public is greedy for mystery.[8]

Theater in the service of the evangelization of culture aims to be an experience in this fullest sense.

The Encounter with the Actor

Why is the theater an appropriate way and place to show original sin? The simple and most compelling answer is because of *the presence of the actors.* I have always been struck by the fact that in his first encyclical, *Redemptor Hominis,* in the very first paragraph of that document, Pope John Paul II wrote, "God entered the history of humanity and, as a man, *became an actor* in that history."[9] Since

7. Giussani, *Risk of Education,* p. 99.

8. Antonin Artaud, *The Theatre Before Its Double,* trans. *Mary Caroline Richards* (New York: Grove Weidenfeld, 1958).

9. John Paul II, Encyclical Letter, *The Redeemer of Man (Redemptor Hominis),* (4 March 1979), n. 1.

Karol Wojtyła had at one time been a theater actor, I cannot help but to think that our late Holy Father chose that term consciously and deliberately, fully mindful of all its implications.

In 2002, John Paul II wrote these words: "Man never stops seeking: both when he is marked by the drama of violence, loneliness, and insignificance, and when he lives in serenity and joy, he continues to seek. The only answer which can satisfy him and appease this search of his comes from the encounter with the One who is at the source of his being and his action."[10] Or to put it in other words, the only thing strong enough to shake us out of our self-satisfaction by which we measure and manipulate reality according to some self-appointed, self-referential idol is a *Presence:* the Presence of Jesus Christ the actor in history. As Giussani expresses it, "That for which the 'I' is made and for which it does everything is a Presence.... It is for a Presence—through which the human being is made, and by which he feels made, and is aware of being made: the presence of Christ . . . that he lives and does everything."[11] The Italian theologian Father Stephano Alberto states:

> All the delusion of our limitation, all the apparent non-keeping of the promise in our fleshly existence, all the desire that decays into utopia and censures the hope because of the burden of our limitation and our pain, finds an answer: it is a Presence, a human Presence. God did not answer the demand for meaning with words, but with a presence.[12]

Look at it this way. When you go to a Broadway play, and you sit down in your seat and open up your playbill, what is the one thing that you dread the most? You dread one of those little square pieces of paper falling out of it. Why? Because those little paper inserts indicate that an understudy is going to be substituting for an actor at

---

10. John Paul II, "Letter to Luigi Giussani, 11 February 22, 2002," *Traces: Communion and Liberation International Magazine,* March 2002.

11. Luigi Giussani, *The Exercises of the Fraternity of Communion and Liberation* (Rimini: Fraternita de comunione e liberatione, 1999), p. 32.

12. Stephano Alberto, *The Exercises of the Fraternity of Communion and Liberation* (Rimini: Fraternita de comunione e liberatione, 2000), p. 29.

that performance. And we're disappointed. But why? The role is still going to be portrayed. Yes, but we came to the theater not only with the hope of encountering this *character* but also this specific *actor.* Because somehow we are convinced that the flesh and blood presence of this particular actor has the power to give life to a given dramatic role in a way that effects an incomparable encounter. We go to the theater to experience an *encounter*—not an encounter only with an "idea," but an encounter with a personal presence that corresponds to something primal and vital in the human soul. In the words of von Balthasar, "the analogy between God's action and the world drama is no mere metaphor but has an ontological ground: the two dramas are not utterly unconnected; there is an inner link between them."[13] Theater in the service of the evangelization of culture recognizes and takes full advantage of the "sacredness" of acting as a participation in God's chosen method of salvation—the Father sent Jesus Christ the actor into human history.

Von Balthasar notes that "theatre owes its very existence substantially to man's need to recognize himself as playing a role."[14] Christ reveals man to himself. As actor reveals the contours of the role of the human "I" in the human drama, so Christ reveals man to himself.

For me, one of the seminal writings on the theater is an essay by the great American playwright Arthur Miller entitled "Tragedy and the Common Man," which he wrote as a foreword to his classic play *Death of a Salesman.* I find the essay monumental because of the innovative and unflinching way that Miller accords the noble status of the tragic hero to the common, ordinary human being. This was something unthinkable in the opinion of Aristotle and others of his ilk, for whom only kings and the high born could be apt tragic heroes. What Miller observed and portrayed in *Death of a Salesman* was what had been confirmed in the coming of the Son of God at the Incarnation and Passion.

13. Von Balthasar, *Theo-drama*, p. 19.
14. Ibid., p. 20.

The human condition in many respects resembles tragedy formally understood. What is it that fuels tragedy? Miller posits that it is "the underlying fear of being displaced, the disaster inherent in being torn away from our chosen image of what and who we are in this world. Among us today this fear is as strong, and perhaps stronger, than it ever was. In fact, it is the common man who knows this fear best."[15] This fact is what makes the common man "as apt a subject for tragedy in its highest sense as kings were."[16] For, he says, "tragedy is the consequence of a man's total compulsion to evaluate himself justly."[17] In the process, "tragedy enlightens—and it must, in that it points the heroic finger at the enemy of man's freedom. The thrust for freedom is the quality in tragedy which exalts."[18] Miller well understands that the only thing that can loose the hold original sin has on us—what makes us fearful of being torn from our chosen image of who we are in the world—is a heroic presence. He says, "The tragic feeling is evoked in us when we are in the presence of a character who is ready to lay down his life, if need be, to secure one thing—his sense of personal dignity."[19] In this perspective, the celebrated "tragic flaw" of the tragic hero is not so much a defect as it is a conviction that results in dire consequences. Miller says that "the 'tragic flaw'" is the hero's "inherent unwillingness to remain passive in the face of what he conceives to be a challenge to his dignity, his image of his rightful status."[20]

Through the exceptional presence of a talented actor who portrays the human compulsion to evaluate himself justly, we, the audience, can face the presence of the tragic hero in ourselves and, with great courage, take up that role in freedom. Theater in the service of the evangelization of culture seeks to promote tragic heroes of just this sort.

15. Arthur Miller, "Tragedy and the Common Man," in *The Theater Essays of Arthur Miller*, ed. Robert A. Martin and Steven R. Centola (New York: Da Capo Press, 1996), p. 5.

16. Miller, "Tragedy," p. 3.   17. Ibid., p. 5.

18. Ibid.   19. Ibid., p. 4.

20. Ibid.

Language: The Medium of Theater

What is the medium that theater employs in order to accomplish its end? The medium of the theater is *language*. Christ comes into the world when the Father speaks the Word. In a removed but real way, theater acts to carry on that Trinitarian utterance. Before all else, plays are meant to be heard. In a unique way, language is ideally suited both to divine self-communication and to theatrical catharsis. For as the then Cardinal Joseph Ratzinger noted, "the conversation between people only comes into its own when they are no longer trying to express something, but *to express themselves*, when dialogue becomes communication."[21] Or, as Giussani has said, affection is the true motive of communication.

As a young man actively involved in a drama project known as the Rhapsodic Theatre, Karol Wojtyła clearly understood and embraced this dimension of language and strove to reconceive theater according to it. He wrote:

> The fundamental element of dramatic art is the living human word. It is also the nucleus of drama, a leaven through which human deeds pass, and from which they derive their proper dynamics. . . . Drama fulfills its social function not so much by demonstrating action as by demonstrating it slowed down, by demonstrating the paths on which it matures in human thought and down which it departs from that thought to express itself externally.[22]

As part of his reflection on his Golden Anniversary of priestly ordination, Pope John Paul II wrote that "the word . . . is present in human history as a fundamental dimension of man's spiritual experience. Ultimately, the mystery of language brings us back *to the inscrutable*

21. Joseph Ratzinger, *Introduction to Christianity*, trans. J. R. Foster and Michael J. Miller (San Francisco: Ignatius Press, 1990), p. 61.

22. Karol Wojtyła, *The Collected Plays and Writings on Theater*, trans. and introduction by Boleslaw Taborski (Berkeley: University of California Press 1987), pp. 379-80.

mystery of God himself."[23] Theater in the service of the evangelization of culture recognizes this crucial truth about language and harnesses it to its fullest effect.

Presence and the Audience

The presence of the audience, also, is absolutely indispensable to theater. Movies can play in an empty movie house to the detriment of no one (except maybe the owner of the movie house!). But the performance of a play in a theater with no audience would cause great sadness to the actors; in fact, it would probably be impossible, for there is a symbiosis between audience and actors that is integral to the theater experience.

There is something wondrous, maybe even mildly miraculous, about an audience leaving the comfort of their own homes to come to a theater. And I cannot help but believe that one reason why they are willing to make the sacrifice to come to the theater is because of this dynamic identified by Giussani's observation, "Meaning is a connection that you establish when you step out of yourself, move out from the instant, and place yourself in a relationship."[24] Becoming an audience is a little way of experiencing *belonging.* I think deep down we know that we need to step out of ourselves in order to establish meaning. I think deep down we are convinced that we need to place ourselves in a relationship—even one as fleeting as the performance of a play—in order to gain the connection which is meaning.

In some concrete way, the act of coming together as an audience tears out of us the nothingness that afflicts all people—what von Balthasar describes as "the sense of being trapped and closed in upon ourselves." Why else would we happily consent to sit in the dark with

23. John Paul II, *Gift and Mystery: On the Fiftieth Anniversary of My Priestly Ordination* (New York: Doubleday, 1996)

24. Luigi Giusanni, *The Religious Sense,* trans. John Zucchi (Montreal & Kingston: McGill-Queen's University Press, 1997), p. 118.

so many strangers and there "willingly suspend disbelief"—to use Samuel Taylor Coleridge's famous phrase—toward what is played out in front of us? The answer is, because the event of theater is not about make-believe but rather about belief-making.

Conclusion

In his *Letter to Artists,* John Paul II writes:

> In situations where culture and the Church are far apart, art remains a kind of bridge to religious experience. . . . Art is by its nature a kind of appeal to the mystery. Even when they explore the darkest depths of the soul or the most unsettling aspects of evil, artists give voice in a way to the universal desire for redemption. . . . The Church is especially. . . . keen that in our own time there be *a new alliance with artists.* . . . I appeal to you, artists of the written and spoken word, *of the theatre* and music. . . . I appeal especially to you, Christian artists: I wish to remind each of you that you are invited to use your creative intuition to enter into the heart of *the mystery of the Incarnate God* and at the same time into *the mystery of man.*[25]

John Paul II reminds us that "unless faith becomes culture it has not been really welcomed, fully lived, humanly rethought." To a great degree, this is the responsibility of the theater in the Church.

25. John Paul II, *Letter to Artists,* 4 April 1999, n. 10; emphasis mine.

five

Guy Bedouelle

CINEMA AND GRACE

What is the cinema? Cinema means a show. Cinema creates an in-dustry. Cinema is an art. Like any show, the cinema must offer diver-sion, supply emotion, and bedazzle us. Cinema can create in us the innocent joys of childhood, but it can also arouse the most primitive of human instincts. Like any industry, cinema falls under the law of economic constraints and under the stricture of corporate or state-sponsored control: cinema passes through a circuit of intermediaries and depends in grand measure on a budget for publicity and distri-bution. (Consider the recent speculation about how Mel Gibson ac-complished these tasks for his independently produced *The Passion of Christ*.) Like all art, cinema can oscillate between kitsch, vulgarity, or banality on the one hand, and on the other, generate chef d'œvres by its creativity and aestheticism. Cinema represents one of the most complete art forms, inasmuch as it integrates photography, music, and even theater, even if film makers do not like to think of themselves as recording what happens on stage. It is also one of the most difficult and expensive art forms on account of the means necessary for its production and technical diffusion. We see then that the cinema presents a complex art form.

Like all complex art forms that incorporate image and sound, cinema has arrived at its maturity The cinema speaks of human nature and addresses itself to man. It thus reaches the spiritual part of us human beings, what in fact makes us members of the race, what constitutes each individual as part of a universal class of beings. To take full account of this specificity and universality belongs to the person who grasps the spiritual dimension of Creation.

The Cinema and the Universal

The universality that the cinema achieves depends first of all on its language, which, even by definition, tries to reach the largest circle of communication possible. In this regard, the communication was absolute during the period of the silent films, that is, without the mediation of words: facial expression itself gave understanding to the most primordial sentiments known to man; everybody was able to recognize love, hate, pity, disdain, affront, admiration—think of Charlot, Charlie Chaplin . . .

The first American films, such as those of David Griffith (and even more so the Soviet cinema with its works by Eisenstein, Poudovkine, and Dovjenko) draw the viewer into an immediate comprehension, which is simple, indeed sometimes *simpliste,* with no more mystery than that achieved by zooming in on a naked face. It was thus that Joan of Arc, particularly in the scene where she receives her last Holy Communion before her execution, appears in Dreyer's 1928 film, "La Passion de Jeanne d'Arc."

With the "talkies," what I have termed "absolute communication" was in a certain way lost, to the extent that the language game complicates and multiplies the relations of the viewer with the film. When in 1961 a Japanese film, *The Naked Island,* by film maker Kaneto Shindo introduced a recovery of silence, the film enjoyed an enormous success. But unlike the original silent films, the cinema today opens our eyes to entire continents, and we are in a position to contemplate them, to hear their native sounds, and indeed to come to love them. Who is better able to present Japan than the adorable art of Ozu or of Mizogushi? Who is able, with more of its ineffable beauty, to make me encounter India and the Bengal than Satyajit Ray?

The adaptation of works of world literature aims also to achieve this broad comprehension of things which is the vocation of the cinema. One is able to admire its powers of adaptation by observing the talent with which Dostoevsky or Shakespeare can be put on the big screen by film makers from Japan, Russia, the United States, and France. Observe that these *cinéastes* do not always choose the greatest works for their film projects. Cervantes' *Don Quixote* or Proust's *La recherche du temps perdu* touched upon the audacious. We find nothing, though, from Dante, nothing from Solzhenitsyn, nothing from the Old Testament either, which after all, more than all the other sacred texts of the human race, contains its share of personages and of violent but also tender stories that make it a candidate for cinematographic transcription. The American super-productions, films in the style of Cecil B. De Mille, never pretended to serve as a true representation. Only Robert Bresson was sufficiently bold to have thought of making a film about the Book of Genesis, but he was forced, for financial reasons, to renounce his good intentions. By contrast, the figure of Christ has inspired many works, for the better, for the average, and for the worse. At the conclusion of this paper, I will briefly discuss Mel Gibson's film *The Passion of Christ.*

The "phenomenon" of the French film maker Bresson, who died in 1997, represents a final challenge to universality of communication by having opened up another and a new debate: Is cinema conceived for an elite, does it require an effort to appreciate, must the viewer first master ground rules, or rather does it belong to the masses? Is cinema for the intellectual swells or for the general public? The answer cannot be simple.

We know that great film makers knew how to keep their works before a large viewership, but they achieved this effect mostly by making people laugh or by producing artificial emotion for its own sake. So it was, without a doubt, with Charlie Chaplin, John Ford, Roberto Rossellini, the Fellini of *La Strada* or *Amarcord,* Alfred Hitchcock, and John Huston. And it was most certainly so with some films of Marcel Carné, René Clair, and Jean Renoir during the high period of French cinema that occurred *entre les deux guerres,* between the two world wars of the twentieth century. In point of fact, I would even include in this category Clint Eastwood: these are all the exceptional artists-authors-creators who united excellence to communication.

The greater number of "film-authors" oscillate between quality films for everybody and films designed to suit a class of intellectuals, called cinephiles, that is, enthusiasts of the cinema. In this case, one is resigned to leave to the ordinary viewing audience the diversionary spectaculars tailored to their particular tastes and interests. Sometimes these spectaculars are executed with intelligence and respect, but more often with mediocrity, not to mention simple buffoonery or pornographic objectification, even when the latter is publicized as "erotic." Some rare film makers have risked trying to reach large audiences without renouncing the quality of their art or of their intellectual principles. Here I would mention Luchino Visconti in his first film, Pier Paolo Pasolini sometimes, and perhaps even Ingmar Bergman in certain of his films. Thus, his 1975 adaptation of Mozart's opera *The Magic Flute* affords an example of a well-thought-out project, indeed a small miracle, achieved through an alliance of artistic subtlety and entertainment: obviously, there is also the magic of the music at work in this example.

One must take account, at this juncture, that this dilemma between sophisticated art and commercial film products occurs in every form of modern art: painting, sculpture, music, dance, theater. These forms, when intellectualized, make their comprehension difficult for the average person. Theater itself, without renouncing its calling to be "popular"—and even at that moment when it protests too much— nonetheless often becomes overly sophisticated.

It behooves us, then, to search the interior dimension of the cinema. We will focus on its proper spiritual sense, rather than only on its technique or its ambition to achieve a universality that would touch both the elite and the everyman. The very subject matter of this art is nothing other than humanity itself.

The Cinema and the Hope of the Human Race

More than any other art, the cinema speaks directly about the human condition, about the human race, about man. It regards the human person in his universe, on his journey of life, and the adventures that living life brings. It would be wrong to imagine that the cinema intends to "deliver a message," clearly discernible, accessible at first flush. Such is not of course forbidden. There have been films made for purposes of propaganda, and film makers either generous or politically engaged produce films with messages that are political, social, or religious. It is not the generosity of these authors that lends credibility to their work, but the quality of their artistic achievement.

Worthy causes require good advocates. True cinema should never descend to the level of a cheap work of moral edification. The most noble cause (for the cinema) remains man himself, from his birth to his death, with an eye always upon his destiny, an eye that is as true as it is attentive, and, to be honest, that is more attentive than merciful. In short, true cinema aims to capture being in its fullness.

Nothing that is of interest to the human person can leave the film maker indifferent. For example, the irruption or evolution of conscience can be slowly observed in exceptional instances such as François Truffaut's 1970 *L'Enfant sauvage,* which displays the true history of a young boy who in the nineteenth century had survived alone in the wild, and who opens up to his humanity in slow motion. In fact, all films that put children—those instinctive actors who are the favorites of audiences—on the silver screen start with their initiation into life, from the description of this marvelous and incomprehensible metamorphosis that we human beings undergo until we reach the age of adulthood. This movement starts at birth.

At the other end of this profile is death, the most profound reality to which art can address itself. Cinema can embrace death without pretense. From Dreyer to Bergman, from Cocteau to Visconti, from Buñuel to Tarkovski, all the great film makers have made death the focus of their cinematographic meditation. It should be not at all astonishing, moreover, that in weaving together the life and the death of man, there emerges the shadow of God or distinct attempts to deny it. An image reflects the one whose image is cast. With Bresson or other film makers who acknowledge Christian inspiration, God speaks, or at least murmurs (which is most often the divine way). But among the majority of authors, only the spiritual thirst of their characters, their nostalgia, their disorders are able to make transparent from a distance what we call the "divine." The "problem," so-called, of God is explicit in the first works of Bergman, even to the point of denial, and it becomes completely absent in the last films of this Swedish film maker, where he attempts to make do with so many declarations of epicurean philosophy—for example, the 1981 *Fanny and Alexander.*

Love constitutes another theme, a predominant one; indeed, a monopolizing and tyrannical one, most often suggested—or even displayed—in its effervescence through the sexual act. Among true film makers, it is neither complacence, nor complicity, nor voyeurism, possessing a surplus of love, of tenderness, of communion in order for man to fulfill himself, or escape isolation, or transcend himself. Spirituality at the movies, the spiritual dimension of the cinema, will take on the form of these tales of human love, of love shared, refused, misunderstood, left out, and found again. There is great nuance found in the history of cinema from the time when a delicate modesty reigned to the cases of extreme sensuality. Think only of the fascinating and at the same time deeply tragic evolution of the Italian film maker Pier Paulo Pasolini, where we witness his original directness, sparkle, and talent become strangled in a cry of despair.

There remains a final element to consider, though it admittedly may be called modern. History has made its way into the cinema, an inauguration genially carried out to be sure by Eisenstein but also by David Griffith, for example in his 1915 *Birth of a Nation*. While often "recuperated," used and badly treated, history ought nonetheless to have its place in the art of the cinema, which cannot shy away from integrating man into time. Perhaps the figure who has understood this truth with the greatest profundity is Andrzej Wajda. This Polish film maker turned a whole series of films devoted to the Polish state and to the great works of its literature, including making films as instruments of resistance to the communist dictatorship, as the great Tarkovski had done up to the point of self-chosen exile.

It is necessary to evoke the moral dimension of humanity, the debates that transpire within us, our self-questioning and our internal paradoxes. In my view, these are found best in the films of another Polish film maker, Christoph Kieslowski, who presents himself as an agnostic, and whose films have best tried to explore, without didactic heaviness, this inevitable confrontation with moral values. You may have seen his ten-part series *The Decalogue*.

Life, death, God or the void, love or refusal to love, time and history: from all of the foregoing emerges the person of human nature, of flesh and blood. Cinema wants to take account of all of these determinations, and from this account move on to the mystery which occupies the human heart.

There exists a strong tradition of cinema criticism—the film critic—most often of Christian inspiration that tries to draw our attention to the spiritual dimensions of the cinema. I wish to name only one critic who has been my *maître*, Henri Agel, at the moment advanced in years, who declared, at the moment when it should have been said, sixty years ago, that the cinema indeed possesses "une âme," . . . a soul. To put it otherwise, more "culturally, or as you would say, politically, correct," there exists a poetic dimension to all cinema. For the poet remains the one who manifests the mystery without destroying it, without violating it, without corrupting it, but by showing it. More specifically, cinema, like poetry, enables a zone of freedom in which readers or viewers discover a receptiveness for interpretation. From this point of view, the function of the critic is not to judge but to communicate, and even to reconcile. We discover then a reciprocity: we are able, with our humble energies, to nourish the works, communicate our life to them. At the same time, they nourish us, and we retrieve our souls.

I am not prepared to go as far as Truffaut, who was bold enough to pose the question: Is cinema more important than life? But I am prepared to give a privileged role to this art form developed during the course of the twentieth century. I do acknowledge that I discover there my true self. Why? Because at the movies, venue of recreation, I am free to discern what the labors or fatigues of daily life habitually keep me from distinguishing all around me, even though I try hard to figure things out.

So, can we say that grace is communicated by the mediation of the cinema? Without a doubt, but in a way that nourishes—in French I would say, "irrigates"—our human existence, the world, and history. Maybe it is better to frame the question differently. Does the cinema teach me to see things more clearly? Does it instruct me about the spiritual dimension of my existence and of those persons who surround me? Does it aid me to discover meaning among the contradictions of the world? Let me put the question more directly:Does a light onto "true life" reach me in the dark recesses of the movie hall? Yes, and that is the spirituality of the cinema.

Turning finally, as I promised, to *The Passion of Christ,* I would like to speak about the film itself and not about *l'affaire* Mel Gibson, that is, the various controversies that have arisen in reaction to the film and to its director. As I did with the works of others who have made films about Christ—Pasolini, who was a communist, Zeffirelli, who is a Catholic, and Rosellini, who was a good-willed agnostic—I look at the film from the point of view of my faith and my sensibility. At the same time, I recognize the personal intention of Mel Gibson, which he himself expressed: "I wanted the effort to be a testament to the infinite love of Jesus the Christ which has saved and continues to save many the world over."

Gibson's "effort," if I understand him well, has been to retrieve an image of Christ that has found a home in Catholic piety and tradition since the end of the Middle Ages. Think about the Franciscans and their devotion to the Stations of the Cross. Think also of the mystery plays—still enacted in places like Oberamergau—and of Baroque images and paintings where the Passion is represented in full color. Then consider the visions of Anne-Catherine Emerich. Gibson wanted to pick up this tradition using the forms of modern-day film of the epic type.

What did I like in the film? First, the ambitious project of putting in the mouths of the actors the languages used in Christ's own time, even if ancient language scholars may dispute one or another detail. This bold effort gives a certain majesty, a strangeness, and thus a distance that is put at the service of the mystery. Second, the skillful use of flashbacks, without which the Passion itself cannot be understood in its full theological sense: for example, to the Last Supper and to the teaching Christ, for example, his Sermon on the Mount. Third, the faces of the characters, and above all that of the Virgin Mary. You noticed that Mary was present throughout the film. I can only conclude that her presence was a theological choice on the part of Mel Gibson. But consider also the faces of the apostles, and those of many other characters: their eyes communicate pity, questioning, of the other and perhaps of themselves, and also a fundamental, deep-down lack of comprehension. Why do I like these faces? Only cinema, as I remarked in my conference, possesses the capacity to display the movements of human expression. This is why I refer to the cinema as the art of the Incarnation. It gives living flesh to a universal mystery. In the case of this film, the mystery is that of the Passion of Christ.

At the same time, I had a few reservations about the film. My first reservation centers on the historical temptations. The way that Mel Gibson directed the religious authorities seemed to me without the kind of nuance that he introduced into the figure of Pilate, especially given the creative interpretation of Pilate's wife, which arguably lacks full justification as far as I am aware. My second reservation centers on his predilection for showing suffering: there was, in my view, too much blood and gore. I understand that Mel Gibson wanted to demonstrate the realism of Christ's Passion, but did he measure sufficiently the inbuilt capacity of the cinema to assault the sensibilities of the audience? (One may also make the same criticism of the ceaseless dramatic music accompanying the action.) If I were to summarize this second reservation, I would say that Mel Gibson forfeited the discreet descriptive balance that one finds in the Gospels themselves.

six

Daniel N. Robinson

CULTURE AND ANARCHY REVISITED

Arnoldian Reflections on Sweetness and Light

What might be called the religious, political, and aesthetic dimensions of the nineteenth century were set by a small army of essayists and the influential journals willing and eager to bring their words to a large and growing middle class. The foundations for this phenomenon were established in the previous century by pamphlets and treatises intended to overturn the settled views and institutional arrangements in place for centuries. The great reform movement in England, which resulted in major parliamentary initiatives in the 1830s, was one product of the intense and even fearful debates engendered by the revolutions in America and in France in the closing decades of the eighteenth century. Now breathing the somewhat intoxicating air of freedom, and the destabilizing effects of the new social mobility, citizens of the New World and the Anglo-European world looked increasingly toward the secular world for guidance. To a degree now difficult to appreciate, effective guidance was provided by any number of periodicals and books, journals and printed sermons, pamphlets and numerous organized societies. Consider only the observation made by John Morely, writing an obituary occasioned by the death of his friend, John Stuart Mill. Morely notes that in Mill's own lifetime, his philosophical treatises sold "for the price of a railway novel," this being the unarguable evidence of the avidity with which ordinary citizens approached major treatises on matters moral, political, and spiritual.

Many names may be recorded among the writers of the period who could claim large followings, but surely the one who spoke with greatest authority on the large question of culture itself—the question of just what must not be lost as the world seeks to liberate itself from the burdens of tradition—was Matthew Arnold (1822–1888). Son of Thomas Arnold, the legendary head of Rugby School, he would be graduated from Balliol College, Oxford and then be made Fellow of Oriel College. Employed for most of his life as Inspector of Schools for the Crown, Arnold early distinguished himself as a poet and literary critic. He served as Professor of Poetry at Oxford for the decade beginning in 1857, but his essays soon moved well beyond literary criticism, reaching to the very foundations of culture itself, and the life it affords—the life it *requires*—when culture itself is properly understood. Abandoned, culture must leave in its wake the nihilism of anarchy which, too, must be understood in terms too subtle and complex for dictionary definitions. Let me move then into the pages of his *Culture and Anarchy,* published in 1869. I will rely at first on a number of passages taken directly from the text in order to have Arnold's voice state Arnold's purposes. I will then move to what I take to be the most important lessons to be drawn by our own age from the diagnosis and therapy Arnold offers to a nineteenth century pursuing that path that, alas, leads to us.

The very first lines of his Preface to the work express Arnold's original intentions for the essay:

My foremost design in writing this Preface is to address a word of exhortation to the Society for Promoting Christian Knowledge. In the essay which follows, the reader will often find Bishop Wilson quoted. To me and to the members of the Society for Promoting Christian Knowledge his name and writings are still, no doubt, familiar; but the world is fast going away from old-fashioned people of his sort.[1]

I must pause to introduce Bishop Wilson (1698–1755) to the audience for, if in 1869 the world had moved away from such a person, in 2009 he must be nearly invisible. And what more appropriate way to revive memories of this exceptional person than to offer these lines by John Henry Newman:

> A burning and shining light was Bishop Wilson; he seemed like the Baptist in an evil time, as if a beacon lighted on his small island to show what his Lord and Saviour could do in spite of man; how when a nation had fallen into the enemies' hands he could preach to it even off its own shores, and be nigh at hand when they would fain leave him not so much as to set his foot on. The English soil, indeed, had its own witnesses and teachers at the time; but none at once so exalted in station and so saintly in character, so active and so tried in his lifetime, and so influential in his works, as Bishop Wilson.[2]

What Matthew Arnold finds in the maxims of Bishop Wilson is the unusual balance of sound common sense, great piety, a realistic appraisal of the possibilities actually afforded by life, and a realistic guide to how one might live this life conformable to Christian ideals. And so, when Arnold moves further into his Preface, he extols the value of Bishop Wilson's works in yet other words, now describing the "the whole scope" of *Culture and Anarchy* as establishing

---

1. Matthew Arnold, "Preface," in *Culture and Anarchy: An Essay in Political and Social Criticism* (New York: Macmillan, 1910), p. vii.

2. From Newman's 1838 preface to Thomas Wilson's *Sacra privata: The Private Meditations, Devotions, and Prayers* (New York: D. Appleton & Co, 1847).

culture as the great help out of our present difficulties; culture being a pursuit of our total perfection by means of getting to know, on all the matters which most concern us, the best which has been thought and said in the world, and, through this knowledge, turning a stream of fresh and free thought upon our stock notions and habits, which we now follow staunchly but mechanically, vainly imagining that there is a virtue in following them staunchly which makes up for the mischief of following them mechanically.[3]

It is the central theme of Arnold's ever timely essay that culture, "is the study of perfection," and that we are to understand

true human perfection as a harmonious perfection, developing all sides of our humanity; and as a general perfection, developing all parts of our society. For if one member suffer, the other members must suffer with it; and the fewer there are that follow the true way of salvation the harder that way is to find.[4]

The theme is that of integration; the integration of faith, reason, beauty, charity, and the courage to take stock of ourselves and recognize the work that needs to be done. It is through the study of perfection itself that one may measure one's own progress, the progress of one's world, against a standard no less real for being ultimately unattainable.

A student of history and of the endeavors that may be said to be mindful of the ideal of perfection, Arnold identifies *religion* as "the greatest and most important of the efforts by which the human race has manifested its impulse to perfect itself."[5] He describes it as "that voice of the deepest human experience."[6] It shares with culture "the aim of setting ourselves to ascertain what perfection is and to make it prevail," seeking to establish "in what human perfection consists."[7] In this latter mission, culture and religion again reach identical conclu-

3. Arnold, "Preface," p. xii.   4. Ibid., p. xiv.
5. Arnold, *Culture and Anarchy*, p. 10.   6. Ibid.
7. Ibid.

sions. Culture comes to its conclusion by way of the voice of human experience as this is recorded in history, poetry, philosophy, the arts and sciences, the study of religion. Religion's conclusion is expressed rather more directly and economically: "The Kingdom of God is within you."[8] This will be central to Arnold's analysis, which understands human perfection to be an *internal* condition, marking what he calls "the growth and predominance of our humanity proper . . . the ever increasing efficaciousness and . . . general harmonious expansion of those gifts of thought and feeling which make the peculiar dignity, wealth, and happiness of human nature."[9]

Perfection thus understood consists in "becoming something rather than in having something, in an inward condition of the mind and spirit, not in an outward set of circumstances."[10] Another passage from this worthy work adds depth and clarity to this picture:

As I have said on a former occasion: "It is in making endless additions to itself, in the endless expansion of its powers, in endless growth in wisdom and beauty, that the spirit of the human race finds its ideal. To reach this ideal, culture is an indispensable aid, and that is the true value of culture."[11]

It is a repeated lesson in *Culture and Anarchy* that the influence of culture, though internal and deeply personal, must finally be found in the general welfare. Recognizing humanity as "one great whole,"[12] Arnold finds in each of us a sympathy, as he calls it, which makes it if not impossible than surely unnatural for any of us to be indifferent to the rest of us, or to think our personal welfare can be isolated from the welfare of others. Thus, he says,

the expansion of our humanity, to suit the idea of perfection which culture forms, must be a general expansion. Perfection, as culture conceives it, is not possible while the individual remains isolated: the

8. Ibid. 9. Ibid., pp. 10–11.
10. Ibid., p. 12. 11. Ibid., p. 11.
12. Ibid.

individual is obliged, under pain of being stunted and enfeebled in his own development if he disobeys, to carry others along with him in his march towards perfection, to be continually doing all he can to enlarge and increase the volume of the human stream sweeping thitherward; and here, once more, it lays on us the same obligation as religion, which says, as Bishop Wilson has admirably put it, that "to promote the kingdom of God is to increase and hasten one's own happiness."[13]

When Arnold calls culture "the great help out of our present difficulties," we may ask just which difficulties he had in mind, and whether our own difficulties are so different as to date this essay. What he sees at the root of the difficulties of his age and his nation is the reliance on what is external and mechanical. Not only is his age devoted to the mechanical and the external—and I will return to these terms—but, owing to its wealth and power, it now exports these values and perspectives everywhere. The devotion to what is finally machinery is reflected not simply in labor-saving devices or toys for persons of all ages. It is grounded in a more fundamental and finally pernicious conviction that the problems of life will have mechanical solutions; solutions arising from formulas and linkages and devices; solutions ready to hand once the machinery of a legislature is engaged, once the pronouncements of a court are widely audible.

Might Arnold be speaking to our own age as well as his own when he says,

> Faith in machinery is, I said, our besetting danger; often in machinery most absurdly disproportioned to the end which this machinery, if it is to do any good at all, is to serve; but always in machinery, as if it had a value in and for itself. What is freedom but machinery? what is population but machinery? what is coal but machinery? what are railroads but machinery? what is wealth but machinery? what are religious organisations but machinery?[14]

13. Ibid., pp. 11–12.
14. Arnold, *Culture and Anarchy*, p. 13.

And just as machinery is used to secure specific and narrow ends, the gospel of the machine comes to define persons themselves, who must soon come to think of one's own individual life as a kind of instrument for securing one's own individual needs and satisfying one's own individual desires. In Arnold's day, the celebration of the individual was as joyous and vocal as it is today, though with results rather less gross. Those who defended all of this were among Arnold's own circle of liberal friends and acquaintances, for it is not liberty that worries Arnold; it is the conversion of a liberty on which perfectionism depends to a mechanical version—a counterfeit version—that is indifferent to just what it is that freedom yields. Consider these lines as Arnold addresses contemporary mantras:

almost every voice in England is accustomed to speak of these things as if they were precious ends in themselves, and therefore had some of the characters of perfection indisputably joined to them. I have once before noticed Mr. Roebuck's stock argument for proving the greatness and happiness of England as she is, and for quite stopping the mouths of all gainsayers. Mr. Roebuck is never weary of reiterating this argument of his, so I do not know why I should be weary of noticing it. "May not every man in England say what he likes?"—Mr. Roebuck perpetually asks; and that, he thinks, is quite sufficient, and when every man may say what he likes, our aspirations ought to be satisfied. But the aspirations of culture, which is the study of perfection, are not satisfied, unless what men say, when they may say what they like, is worth saying,—has good in it, and more good than bad. In the same way The Times, replying to some foreign strictures on the dress, looks, and behaviour of the English abroad, urges that the English ideal is that every one should be free to do and to look just as he likes. But culture indefatigably tries, not to make what each raw person may like, the rule by which he fashions himself; but to draw ever nearer to a sense of what is indeed beautiful, graceful, and becoming, and to get the raw person to like that.[15]

15. Ibid., p. 14.

Arnold knows that, contrary to the dominant rhetoric of his time, the greatness of England arises not from coal. Greatness, he says, "is a spiritual condition"[16] which surely could survive the disappearance of coal! Consider a catastrophe that finds all of England submerged to the floor of the ocean but with posterity in possession of just what England had produced. Does anyone think that what would excite love, admiration, and interest would be the once-great supplies of coal? Would the age of coal eclipse the Elizabethan Age? Would the railroad summon a degree of attention greater than the works of Shakespeare?

I offer these as a sample of the questions that might be raised when testing the power of an age to engage our attention and lay claims to our respect. Arnold puts all this in the form of Culture now personified and asking a question that we might ask about ourselves and our own age. Culture says,

> Consider these people, then, their way of life, their habits, their manners, the very tones of their voice; look at them attentively; observe the literature they read, the things which give them pleasure, the words which come forth out of their mouths, the thoughts which make the furniture of their minds; would any amount of wealth be worth having with the condition that one was to become just like these people by having it?[17]

Culture is not indifferent to health and appearance, but it does not regard them in the mechanical, functional manner that now dominates our national consciousness. Arnold repeats lines from the Epistle to Timothy: "Bodily exercise profiteth little; but godliness is profitable unto all things."[18] The aim of culture is, in the words of Epictetus, "the formation of the spirit and character,"[19] the formation of what the Greeks called *euphuia*—that "finally tempered nature" which Jonathan Swift reduces to what he calls "the two noblest of things ... *sweetness and light.*"[20]

---

16. Ibid., p. 15.   17. Ibid., p. 16.

18. Ibid., p. 17.   19. Ibid., p. 18.

20. Jonathan Swift, "The Battle of the Books," in *The Tale of a Tub and Other Works* (Kila, MT: Kessinger Publishing, 2005), p. 168.

I will offer no further quotations from *Culture and Anarchy*, but will turn attention now directly to our own age, to our version of faith in machinery, to our own version of individualism. And, in agreement with Arnold, I will suggest that our age has created great difficulties for us, and that the guide to the location of these difficulties and, yes, the way to be relieved of them, is that twin guide, culture and religion, both sharing the aspiration to perfection, both looking within the spirit of the person, both comprehending the real limits of machinery.

First, on this matter of "machinery," let us recognize that Arnold's sense of the term is not confined to physical objects. There are mechanical modes of thought and of action, mechanical modes even of sentiment and desire. I would say that addictive behavior is, in its way, evidence of utterly "mechanized" desires, just as inauthentic expressions of friendship or collegiality are mechanized expressions of decorum. Indeed, what is mindlessly habitual is "mechanical" in that no element of the ideal of perfection is included. Truth be told, there are mechanical forms of worship, mechanical modes of belief, so unaffected by a thoughtful consideration of the meaning of faith, so aloof to needs of the world or the goodness of others as to answer to that very damning criticism, "empty ritual."

Of the mechanical modes of thought, consider how today's psychological thought tends to embrace its proper subject. Consider the reductive strategies that would explain the yearnings and achievements of the world, the sins and errors of the world in terms of one or another event in the brain, one or another chance occurrence in the genetic lottery. So little room is left for the influence of authentic, personal choice—for sincere and carefully framed possibilities for a life to be lived—that the discipline of psychology as a whole really has no methods available with which even to address such matters.

And now consider the arts and the dominant forms of entertainment. Before taking this up, it is useful to look back in time to a world clearly less mechanical, clearly more directly in contact with the realities of life. I refer to the world of the Hellenes, whose tragedians composed plays of depth, subtlety, and power; plays that put us all on notice, presented us with truer pictures of the wages of vice and villainy, and tormented us with the dread news that, try as we may, our lives must finally answer to powers beyond our ken. What I would note about the works of Euripides, Aeschylus and Sophocles is that their creations were the stock—can one even use the word "entertainment"?—were the *moving icons* of the Hellenic world. Contrast this, with its insistent demands on our intelligence, empathy, seriousness, against the stock icons of our own time. The very comparison is impossible, for the two worlds in these respects have nearly nothing in common. One of the two summons its audience to weigh how fallen we are, how vulnerable, yet, with great effort of will and of piety, we may produce an Antigone.

Now think of our architecture, the very "look" of our businesses and our residences. We are supposed to be proud of discovering something oddly called "functionalism," as if that answered any important question or settled a dispute worth having. The notion of "function" is an empty one until the goals and aspirations, the desires and hopes, the problems and the promise, have been identified. Is a hammer "functional"? Surely not as a writing instrument. If what we seek most earnestly is inward perfection, the disposition of sweetness that inclines our efforts toward the best interests of others, and the benefit of that light that grows with our knowledge and our regular association with the best things said and done by the human race—if this is what we seek, then what is "functional" is what serves such ends.

Culture is the study of perfection. Religion, when it is pure and grounded in teachings that take seriously the very nature of human nature and its staggering potential for good and for ill, is a guide to perfection, a measure of our slow and ever-incomplete progress toward it. It is no accident that the greatest of cultural achievements tend to be either inextricably connected to, or the manifest gifts of, or the loftiest ornaments of, a living faith. That civilization that we routinely refer to as "Western"—though moral and aesthetic and civic truths admit of no boundaries—was but the most visible, audible, and legible gift of Christianity, and especially its Roman Catholic form. Under the aegis of the Church, the European continent would be enriched by the first true universities; by the dissemination of Roman law with its organizing and civilizing influence; the patronage of artists and architects, writers and composers, teachers and kings, assembled finally to offer one great, sustained prayer of thanks to the providential and loving God who saw fit to allow a rational animal an opportunity to gain eternal peace and joy.

An age that thinks in a mechanical way tends to take things apart and soon loses the capacity to comprehend them in their wholeness. Thus do many of today's leaders of thought think—and lead others to think—that one might continue to enjoy the benefits of Western civilization while remaining a polite or even not so polite distance from its animating source and its veritable *raison d'être;* as if one might have the justice, and even the mercy, without any reference to sweetness and light; as if, in the name of "freedom," one might permit entire throngs of children to speak rudely and poorly, to look at what is vile, to listen to what is vile, all the while believing that, just as long as their "freedom" is kept intact, we are true to the very traditions that gave rise to freedom itself.

"Feed my sheep" was the master's command to his disciples. Yes, of course the command includes food and shelter and such care as we might extend to those in need. But there is much more to it than this, for to feed the sheep one must know what is essential about them; not only what will sustain life, but what will enrich it and have it realize ever more fully what in its essence is possible. The record of human history indicates that there are, indeed, possibilities far beyond those of a merely happy life, a merely happy life of individual freedom; possibilities that extend very far beyond the right to say and wear what one wants. The greatest cultural creations alert us to the forms of perfection itself and point to a reality beyond our earthly senses, beyond our earthly wisdom. As the greatest cultural creations point to all this, a true religion will lead one toward it.

The words of Thomas Aquinas express far more clearly what I suggest here. It is in Question LXII of the First Part of the Second Part of the *Summa* that Thomas discusses the Theological Virtues and, in the Third Article, asks whether Faith, Hope, and Charity are properly regarded as theological virtues. Listen to his reply to the objection that faith is less than a virtue, for it is but *imperfect knowledge:* Thomas says,

> Faith and hope imply a certain imperfection: since faith is of things unseen, and hope of things not possessed. Hence, faith and hope in things that are subject to human power fall short of the notion of virtue. But faith and hope in things which are above the capacity of human nature surpass all virtue . . .[21]

This is the wedding of religion and culture, each reaching for what is above the capacity of human nature, if only to keep us mindful that there is, indeed, something transcendent, limitless in knowledge, limitless in love, limitless in sweetness and light.

21. Thomas Aquinas, *Summa theologiae* I-II, q. 62, a. 3.

seven

Stanley Hauerwas

POLITICS AND BEING A CHRISTIAN

1. On Being a Sectarian, Fideistic, Tribalist

I have a well-deserved reputation for being an unapologetic Enlightenment basher. I do not believe something called ethics can be shown to exist or to be justified on Kantian-like grounds of reason alone. I have no use for moral or political liberalism in any of their guises. I do not believe in inalienable rights. I tire of the ongoing futile project to show that freedom of the individual can be reconciled with equality. I do not even believe that a good society can or should be egalitarian if that means all hierarchical considerations bear the burden of proof. Accordingly, many of my colleagues in that strange field called Christian ethics suggest I am a sectarian, fideistic, tribalist.

By this they mean I am trying to convince Christians that we do not have a stake in the "wider world." My oft-made claim, that the first task of Christians is not to make the world more just but rather is to make the world the world, is interpreted as a call for Christians to withdraw from the world—or at least America. That I should be so understood by those working in Christian ethics is quite intelligible if, as I have argued elsewhere, the subject of Christian ethics in America has always been America. Christian ethicists no longer think, as Walter Rauschenbusch did, that their task is to Christianize the social order, but they continue to share Rauschenbusch's presumption that America is the appropriate subject for Christian ethical reflection and action. My refusal to accept this presumption means I cannot help but be interpreted as a traitor to my class or, at least, my discipline.

I confess I have been tempted, and no doubt at times have succumbed to the temptation, to continue to criticize American liberalism in a manner that only confirms such characterizations of my position. Yet I confess I have grown weary of that game. I simply cannot muster energy for yet one more attempt to show the incoherence of liberal political philosophy or practice. Liberalism, both politically and economically, is doing such a good job of self-destructing, it needs no help from me. More important, such a tactic theologically manifests a lack of faith. I believe that the American experiment, as some like to put it, is in deep trouble. Yet Christians are obligated to be a people of hope, not wishing for the lives of our non-Christian brothers and sisters to be worse than they need to be.

Some years ago I wrote an article entitled "A Tale of Two Stories: On Being a Christian and a Texan."[1] I wrote the article mainly to please myself and to honor my parents, but also in response to the oft-made criticism that I failed to appreciate that Christians are constituted by stories other than the Christian story—a point a Texan is not likely to overlook. However, I confess, my self-description as a Texan was insufficient. I am also an American. As much as I might like—as

1. "A Tale of Two Stories: On Being a Christian and a Texan," in my *Christian Existence Today: Essays on Church, World, and Living in Between* (Durham, NC: Labyrinth Press, 1988), pp. 25–45.

a Texan or as a Christian—to deny or avoid that I am an American, I know that any such denial would be self-deceptive. Even more important, I have to acknowledge I love the land and the people called American. Of course, the issue is not my love of America, but rather how such a love should be shaped and governed by the love of God.

So I should like to take this as an opportunity to explore in a more constructive way than is my "normal mode" what positive role the church might have in the project called America. Contrary to the critics of my position, I have no wish to have Christians withdraw from service to their neighbors, even their liberal neighbors. The object of my criticism of liberalism has never been liberals per se, but rather Christians. I have sought to give Christians renewed confidence in the convictions that make our service intelligible. In short, I have never sought to justify Christian withdrawal from social and political involvement; I have just wanted us to be involved as Christians.

From my perspective the problem is not liberalism, but the assumption on the part of many Christians that they must become liberals in order to be of service in America. When that happens I believe Christians betray their non-Christian neighbors because we rob them and ourselves of exemplification of truthful speech forged through the worship of God. What follows is my attempt to suggest what I take to be some mistaken strategies for the negotiation of America by Christians. My criticism of these strategies, however, is meant to make intelligible my claim that Christians have no service more important than to be a people capable of the truthful worship of God.

2. The Problem with the Search for Foundations

I noted above that the subject of Christian ethics in America was America.[2] The birth as well as the intelligibility of Christian ethics as

2. For a more developed account of this theme see my "Why Christian Ethics Is Such a Bad Idea," in *Beyond Mere Health: Theology and Health Care in a Secular Society*, ed. Hilary Regan, Rodney Horsfield, and Gabrielle MacMullen (Melbourne: Australian

a discipline drew on institutions we now call mainstream Protestant Christianity. These churches assumed a deep compatibility between Christianity and American democracy. For most members of such churches, it was unthinkable that being a Christian might in any way render problematic their full participation in American life. Christian ethics accordingly was understood as that mode of reflection that helped churches develop policies to make American ideals of freedom and equality more fully institutionalized in American life.

For both internal and external reasons Christian thinkers learned, as I suggested above, not to describe their task as Christianizing the social order. The appeals of the Social Gospel movement to Jesus, as well as that movement's optimism about progress, were subjected to the withering critique of Reinhold Niebuhr. For Niebuhr, the Christian ethical problem became how to achieve relative justice in a world in which love can never be realized. Though Niebuhr understood himself to be a theologian, or at least a social ethicist, his work is almost completely devoid of any account of the church.[3] Yet I think it also true to say that he continued to assume the viability of Protestant

---

Theological Forum, 1996), pp. 64–79, and "Christian Ethics in America (and the *JRE*): A Report on a Book I Will Not Write," *Journal of Religious Ethics* 25/3 (25th Anniversary Supplement, 1998): 57–76.

3. It is not just that Niebuhr had no or little role for the church in his thought; beyond that, the status of his theological claims is by no means clear. In an extraordinary paragraph in the Preface to the 1964 edition of *The Nature and Destiny of Man* (Louisville: Westminster/John Knox, 1996) Niebuhr observes about his book, "I placed a special emphasis on the eschatology of the New Testament with its special symbols of the Christ and anti-Christ, taking them as symbols of the fact that both good and evil grow in history, and that evil has no separate history, but that a greater evil is always a corruption of a greater good. I believe that the perils of a nuclear age substantiate this interpretation much more vividly than I expected when I presented the thesis. But I am now not so sure that the historic symbols will contribute much to the understanding by modern man of his tragic and ironic history with its refutation of the messianic and utopian hopes of the Renaissance and Enlightenment" (p. xxvi). That Christ only stands on the edge of history was always clear in Niebuhr's work, but that you may not need even the "symbol" is something else again. Interpreting as charitably as possible, one must assume that this observation is not about Christ, but rather the "understanding by modern man."

Christianity as the background for the stance he developed toward social problems. Such an assumption, of course, has become increasingly problematic.

The problematic nature of this project is not due to the increasing loss of membership, social status, and political power of mainstream Christianity. No doubt such losses are not unimportant for understanding the loss of a distinctive voice of Protestant Christianity in America. Yet I think more important has been the increasing recognition that, even if such churches remained socially and politically powerful, they would have nothing distinctive to say as Christians about the challenges facing this society. That such churches have nothing distinctive to contribute is not surprising, since their social and political power originally derived from the presumption that there was no essential difference between the church and the principles of the American experiment. That presumption may, of course, also help explain the decline of such churches, because it is by no means clear why you need to go to church when your church only reinforces what you already know from participation in a democratic society.

The increasing loss of social and political influence of Protestant Christianity has not meant Christian theologians and ethicists have abandoned the attempt to make America correspond to some assumed ideal. Faced, however, with America's increasingly diverse population, their endeavor has been disciplined by the assumption that when Christians enter the public realm they cannot use Christian language. Rather, some mediating language is required and assumed to be justified in the name of a common morality or by natural law reasoning. For those who remain in the tradition of mainstream Protestantism, this often takes the form of trying to show that Rawls, or some Rawls-like account of justice, is the kind of bridge Christians need to justify our participation in the formulation of public policies necessary to govern a diverse society.[4]

4. See, for example, Edmund Santurri, "Rawlsian Liberalism, Moral Truth, and Augustinian Politics," *Journal for Peace and Justice Studies* 8/2 (1997): 1–36. Santurri

I do not intend to be drawn into debates concerning the adequacy of Rawls's account of justice. Yet I want to make clear why the attempt to use Rawls for developing a way for Christians politically to participate in America distracts us from understanding as Christians the contribution we might make. Nicholas Wolterstorff provides a trenchant analysis of Rawls that makes clear why Rawls is such a distraction. As Wolterstorff notes, Rawls thinks a basis for constitutional democracies is necessary because political issues remain contested in our society. For example, it is not clear how liberty and equality can be expressed in the basic rights and liberties of citizens in a manner that answers the claims of both liberty and equality. From Wolterstorff's perspective, Rawls seeks a way to resolve the conflict in the American tradition between Locke and Rousseau—that is, between freedom and equality—by offering his two principles of justice based on common human reason.

Yet Wolterstorff asks how one can possibly move from

> a tradition with internal unresolved conflicts, to a pair of principles which resolves those conflicts, by doing nothing other than analyzing that tradition and elaborating the principles embedded therein? How can common human reason, exercised reasonably, propel one across the chasm separating unresolved conflicts from proposals for resolution? The essence of Rawls' strategy is to make do with our common human reason working on the public political culture of our constitutional democracies. Nothing more than that. Of course analysis and elaboration can in principle clarify for us the content and contours of our public political culture. But if there's conflict in our public political culture as to the relative weighting of liberty and equality, then the application of "our common human reason" to this culture will

---

argues that Christians have a stake in a Rawlsian political strategy to the extent the latter can be saved from Rorty-like skepticism by providing an Augustinian justification. Yet the truth Santurri thinks Augustine supplies is that "order is better than disorder." I find it hard to understand why Augustine is thought necessary to sustain that "truth." Santurri's article is followed by commentaries by David Dawson, Jean Elshtain, Timothy Jackson, Gilbert Meilaender, and Michael White.

make clear to us that there is this conflict. It won't yield a proposal as to how they *ought to be* weighted—unless, perchance, our common human reason is a source of moral principles. But that's the Lockian view which Rawls is trying to avoid, by proposing to extract the relevant moral principles from the extant culture rather than from Reason. If the culture is of different minds as to the relative weighting of liberty and equality, then any proposal as to how they *ought* to be weighted will perforce go beyond what can be extracted from that culture itself.[5]

Wolterstorff concludes—rightly, I think, and contrary to Rawls's conclusion—that we must learn to carry on in a politics that has no foundation. We shall have to conduct our political deliberations without a shared political basis—that is, without a neutral or coherent set of principles sufficient to adjudicate conflicts. This means, according to Wolterstorff, our best strategy is to move from one set of deliberations to another, employing whatever set of considerations we think may be persuasive for the persons with whom we are in conversation. A Rawlsian political unity of overlapping consensus is neither possible nor desirable. All we need, though (Wolterstorff argues), is the unity that

> emerges from dialogue among persons each of whom approaches the dialogue with his or her own distinct frame of conviction, and each of whom is willing to live within the confines of a democratic constitution and with the results of fair votes. That's all the unity we have ever had, in these constitutional democracies of ours characterized by religious, moral, and philosophical pluralism. We don't need, and have never had, an ever-present, never-changing foundation on which all of us who are "reasonable" agree and on the basis of which all of us conduct our deliberations. . . . Agreement must be wrought ever anew in ever new ways among ever new parties. For

5. Nicholas Wolterstorff, *From Presence to Practice: Mind, World, and Entitlement to Believe,* The Gifford Lectures for 1994–95 at the University of St. Andrews. I am indebted to Professor Wolterstorff for making his manuscript available to me. The quote appears on p. 353 of the manuscript.

two hundred years now that's been enough for the endurance of pluralistic constitutional democracies. We have no guarantee that it will
prove sufficient on into the distant future. Only hope.[6]

I believe one of the great advantages of Wolterstorff's way of understanding our situation is this: it does not ask Christians to learn
some third language in order socially and politically to participate
in America. If ours is a "pluralist" society, a description I find far
too complimentary, then I see no reason that Christians (any more
than Jews or secularists) should be asked to put their convictions in
some allegedly neutral language in order to talk with others (non-
Christians) in the society. Of course "talk with others" may be a far
too innocent way to put the matter, in the light of controversies such
as those about abortion and assisted suicide. The problem is not that
we do not talk with one another, but that such talk makes no difference. Yet we will make little progress in even finding our disagreements as long as we search for a "foundation" assumed to be necessary before the conversation begins.

3. On Telling the American Stories

A more promising way to begin to think about how Christians
might contribute to the ongoing American project is that proposed by
Martin Marty in his book *The One and the Many: America's Struggle
for the Common Good.*[7] That Marty is a historian rather than a philosopher is why I find the account he provides promising. Rather than
looking for foundations, he directs our attention to the stories that
constitute the life of that strange entity called America. In this respect
he develops a strand of Christian reflection exemplified in H. Richard
Niebuhr's *The Kingdom of God in America,* Reinhold Niebuhr's *The
Irony of American History,* and the work of Robert Bellah.

6. Wolterstorff, *From Presence to Practice,* p. 358.
7. Martin Marty, *The One and the Many: America's Struggle for the Common Good*
(Cambridge: Harvard University Press, 1997).

(No matter how Bellah has tried to distance himself from his early work on the civil religion of America, I believe it is to his credit that the kind of analysis he and his colleagues provided in *Habits of the Heart* as well as *The Good Society* is in moral continuity with his attempt to name the American civil religion. Bellah's passion has been the attempt to discover the story or stories that can make our common as well as our individual lives as Americans morally good.)

One of the virtues of approaches like those of Bellah and Marty is that they have the potential to take account of aspects of American life that are morally richer than liberal theory can account for. It is often suggested, for example, that liberalism has worked in America exactly because it has been parasitic on forms of life for which liberalism takes no responsibility or may even undermine, such as generosity. Marty's focus on the narratives that constitute our lives is a more promising way, I believe, to exemplify the generous character of America's voice.

That I find these historical and sociological approaches more promising for articulating how Christians might make a contribution in the American context does not mean I agree with what Marty takes that contribution to be. To his credit, Marty has discovered Alasdair MacIntyre. Not only does Marty credit MacIntyre for helping us see how important it is that we discover the narratives we inhabit, but he also takes seriously MacIntyre's judgment that "many citizens in their various competitive groups do inhabit incommensurable universes of discourse, universes that lack a basis of comparison and hence an ability to communicate."[8] Yet Marty thinks MacIntyre's pessimism can be countered by drawing on Felix Frankfurter's contention that this society is not held together by law, creed, or ideology, but by sentiment.

Marty quotes Frankfurter to the effect that "the ultimate foundation of a free society is the binding tie of cohesive sentiment," and observes that such sentiment remains available for us even today in our multicultural society.[9] Indeed Marty, the great celebrator of America,

8. Ibid., pp. 71–72.   9. Ibid., p. 22.

has taken to heart the increasing sense that America is not constituted by one story. Accordingly he criticizes Jefferson and the other founders for using the ideology of the Enlightenment to produce sameness and repress difference. In particular he criticizes the development of the "common school" as well as the texts used in those schools for the repression of difference in the name of creating a common culture. Yet Marty cannot bring himself to abandon the attempt to create a common "sentiment" through what he calls the "commensurable possibilities in storytelling."[10]

He thinks the creation of a common sentiment possible if we learn to think of the nation less as a community and more in terms of Michael Oakeshott's understanding of a "civil association."[11] An association does not demand a credal bond or personal intimacy, but rather requires us, like porcupines, to stand at a distance from one another learning the delight in the other that only the distance can produce. Drawing on the work of the Calvinist social theorist Althusius, Marty suggests that we best understand a commonwealth not as a community of communities but rather as an association of associations. This understanding would allow people in various groups to live in partly incommensurable universes of discourse and yet find it valuable to interact in ways other than through military force and cultural conflict. Rather than reaching for guns, people will learn to "reach for argument, and the telling of stories from different perspectives is a form of argument. One cannot have a republic without argument."[12]

Marty's story remains the optimistic story of America. He expects the conflicts to continue, but believes that in the longer future,

> Every story well told, well heard, and creatively enacted will contribute to the common good and make possible the deepening of values, virtues, and conversation. At the outset I described this book as an effort to contribute to the restoration of the body politic, or, with the many groups in view, the bodies politic. We have been speaking

10. Ibid., pp. 74–76.   11. Ibid., pp. 120–29.
12. Ibid., p. 154.

throughout of the "re-storying" of the republic and its associations. The advice for every citizen who wishes to participate in American life and its necessary arguments: start associating, telling, hearing, and keep talking.[13]

In short, Marty seems to think all this will work out if we just learn to be nice to one another.

Whatever one may think about the strength and/or weakness of Marty's account, what I find striking is the absence of any theological justification. Marty, like Reinhold Niebuhr, assumes his task is making America work. The story Marty tells is the story of America in which Christians get to have a role. That such is the case should not be surprising, since Marty represents the discipline of American religious history. Accordingly, it never seems to occur to him that he needs to tell the church's story of America. As a result, he fails to see how the story of America can tempt Christians to lose our own story and in the process to fail to notice that the god we worship is no longer the God of Israel.

In this respect it is fascinating to compare Marty's account of the challenges before American life with MacIntyre's reading of America. What Marty finds admirable about American life—that is, our desire to get along by being likable people—MacIntyre finds our greatest defect. MacIntyre observes:

> This wanting to be liked is one of the great American vices that emerges from this refusal of particularity and conflict. Americans tend under the influence of this vice to turn into parodies of themselves—smiling, earnest, very kind, generous, nice people, who do terrible things quite inexplicably. We become people with no depth, no depth of understanding, masters of technique and technology but not of ourselves. Colonel Tuan of the Army of the Republic of Vietnam, which we so generously aided and then so treacherously betrayed, was once asked by Paul Theroux what he thought of the Americans. He called them "well-disciplined" and "generous." "But we also think

13. Ibid., p. 225.

that they are a people without culture . . ." He did not mean by this that they lacked high culture. He meant that he could not recognize what it was about them that made them Americans in the way that he was Vietnamese. And that I think is what happens to people with no story to tell of themselves, people who do not confront their future as a narrative future. They, or rather we, become superficial people, people with surfaces, public relations people.[14]

From MacIntyre's perspective, Marty's account of the role of stories but reproduces the liberal presumption that the "good thing" about America is how being an American makes you aware of, and alienates you from, your story.[15] That is why for MacIntyre what he calls "the American idea" cannot help but be tragic. It is tragic because the conflict between the basic American principles of every man to live, to be free, and to pursue happiness cannot be reconciled with the demand for equality. Slavery is but the most obvious contradiction of the American dilemma. According to MacIntyre this contradiction represents a conflict so

> deeply embodied in the American character that no care for a surface appearance of consistency or a superficial disguise for hypocrisy could have got rid of it. It is the contradiction between a profound commitment to the principles of equal rights and liberty on the one hand and an equally profound commitment to individualistic practices which generate inequality and unfreedom on the other. American history is the tragic working out of this internalized contradiction.[16]

---

14. Alasdair MacIntyre, "How to Be a North American" (Washington, D.C.: Federation of State Humanities Councils, 1987), p. 16.

15. I originally thought I might use this paper to explore the difference between the hyphens, that is, the difference between what it means to be, for example, a German-American and a Christian-German and/or American. That America alienates us from our story of origin is not unique, because so does Christianity. Indeed, I suspect one of the problems for Christians in America is the temptation to confuse those two quite different alienations.

16. MacIntyre, "The American Idea," in *America and Ireland, 1976-1996: The American Identity and the Irish Connection*, ed. David Noel Doyle and Owen Dudley Edwards

Marty regrets the general tendency in America for historical amnesia, but he fails to see that a loss of memory is at the heart of the American project. Indeed, as I suggested above, Rawlsian strategies for securing justice require just such a loss of memory. Justice requires the presumption that a genuine break with the past is possible. That is why MacIntyre suggests that America is not just a country, but a metaphysical entity, "an intelligible abstraction always imperfectly embodied in natural reality. It is always *not yet,* it is always radically incomplete; and because the values it aspires to incarnate were from the first seen as *the* essential values, anyone and everyone may be summoned to take part in that completion."[17] Thus America was the attempt to found a historical tradition to connect a particular past to a universal future,

> a tradition that in becoming genuinely universal could find a place within itself for all other particularities so that the Irishman or the Jew or the Japanese in becoming an American did not cease thereby to be something of an Irishman or a Jew or a Japanese. In assuming the burden of this task America took unto itself a genuinely Utopian quality, the quality of an attempt to transcend the limits of secular possibility. America's failures are intimately connected with this grasping after impossibility; but so are its successes.[18]

(Westport, CT: Greenwood Press, 1980), pp. 57–68. This article and "How to Be a North American" need to be more widely known, as they would make easy dismissals of MacIntyre's philosophical arguments much more difficult.

17. MacIntyre, "The American Idea," p. 61. I should note that MacIntyre makes clear that what he calls the American idea is not a single or unitary reality, but presents very different aspects from different points of view and at different times.

18. MacIntyre, "The American Idea," p. 66. MacIntyre cites as "successes" the increase of the number of Americans who graduate from high school, the number of African-Americans who graduate from college, and the availability of health care to the poor.

MacIntyre is, also, particularly critical of those forms of anti-Americanism, characteristic of Europeans, that seek to make America the scapegoat for the sins of Western modernity. Such anti-Americanism is a sign of failure to recognize that in the "democracies of the West you cannot reject America because in the end, if you are honest,

The tragic character of American history is unavoidable, since rights cannot help but conflict with rights; yet the very moral commitments that shape such a conflict produce a people incapable of recognizing, much less responding to, such conflicts. America is at once the name of an aspiration to liberty and equality of rights and the name of the power that stands in the way of that aspiration. As a result, Americans find themselves at war not only with one another but with themselves. MacIntyre observes that "citizens of other nations are free to measure what their government and society does by *external* standards of liberty and right and can choose between their loyalty to these absolutes and their loyalty to their own nature; but the American finds that these absolutes *are* his constitution, that he cannot disown his national allegiance without disowning these moral absolutes or vise versa."[19]

Nothing that MacIntyre has said about America requires him to deny Marty's sense that we need a shared history.[20] MacIntyre doubts we can look to academic historians to supply us with such a story just to the extent that such a history, through its elimination of evaluative judgments, of heroes and heroines, seeks to abolish history as a

---

America is you. Every American has two nationalities, his own and that from which his or her ancestors originally sprang, whether in Europe, Asia, Africa, or in North America itself. But the counterpart to this is that free persons anywhere also have two nations, whether they like it or not—their own and the United States" (p. 68). MacIntyre is not suggesting, I think, that this is a "good thing," but rather that this is the way things are. As I suggested above, the way America alienates us from our origin is quite interestingly compared to how becoming a Christian alienates us from our past. I think the difference is quite simple—the church is not a utopian possibility but a concrete community across time.

19. MacIntyre, "The American Idea," p. 61.

20. The "we," of course, needs to be specified. MacIntyre maintains that the boundaries of a culture cannot be identified with political boundaries. This is particularly important for Americans, since we must realize that "there is no adequate way of telling our common story unless we understand how to relate to Mexican understandings of Mexican history and to Canadian understandings of Canadian history, whether of Quebecois or of English-speaking Canadians" ("How to Be a North American," p. 14).

story.[21] Our problem is that such history, as well as our political culture, has made us quite literally speechless (though of course we go on talking, but such talking represents no more than the clash of opinion). In a striking illustration, MacIntyre offers one exception to our inability to create a common story through public speech—the Vietnam War Memorial. The "Memorial is significant because it both records the names of the dead and also, by style and substance, says that we do not know what to say to or about them. It is a monument to inarticulateness; *both* to our not knowing what to say to and about the dead now, except that they are our dead and dead because of us, *and* to our inarticulateness at the time of the Vietnam war."[22]

MacIntyre acknowledges that it may seem odd to speak of inarticulateness at the time of Vietnam, since so much was said at that time.

21. For a fascinating argument to reclaim history as a moral enterprise, see David Harlan, *The Degradation of American History* (Chicago: University of Chicago Press, 1997). Harlan notes: "American culture cannot be thought of as a single conversation carried on by a limited number of distinct and autonomous voices. It is not, as the champions of multiculturalism contend, that American culture has become too pluralistic and diversified to carry on such a conversation—as if we had become a collection of isolated, marginalized, and exotically distinct subcultures, each one speaking its own private language. In fact, it is pretty much the opposite, for all those putatively distinct subcultures have actually been commingling in the night, combining and coalescing with an unrelenting ferocity . . . This is the point at which Eliot and even Oakeshott fail us. If we are to have the predecessors we need, we must find them ourselves—find them and arrange them such that we can see ourselves as the latest in a long sequence or tradition of such thinkers" (pp. 206-7). That is the task of history, according to Harlan. He is quite pessimistic that history as a social science is capable of such a role.

22. MacIntyre, "How to Be a North American," p. 18. MacIntyre is surely right to praise the Vietnam War Memorial, but I think much more can be said about the monument's significance. That the monument pulls us into itself while we see ourselves reflected in the black marble is surely a representation of how we were drawn into the war. Most of us were spectators to the deaths of those whose names are now on the wall. It is right therefore to see ourselves reflected in their deaths. Moreover the long, slow, path out of Vietnam mimics the long, slow, path into the war. That the monument is, moreover, a slash into the earth is not accidental. The blood spilled in Vietnam by American and Vietnamese surely cries out to us from the ground itself. It is the voice of Abel. Of course such a reading of the memorial is made possible by the Bible. MacIntyre has no reason to resist such a reading, though others might.

Yet he argues that we spoke at such length because we could not communicate. The war simply revealed, therefore, that we were not able to speak intelligibly to each other on matters that were so deep. And, of course, it is exactly such inability that we have worked hard to forget by consoling ourselves with rhetoric of consensus and pluralism. Thus projects such as Marty's mask our loss of shared political speech as well as our lack of communal imagination, "deprivations closely related to our inability to master and to make our own the narrative of ourselves."[23] Shared sentiment cannot help but be sentimental without a more determinative narrative that helps name the truth, the tragic truth, that America is constituted by wrongs so wrong that nothing can be done to make them right.[24]

4. God and America

If you are schooled in the art of revivals, that should make you attentive to the religious payoff here. For if the analysis I have provided is close to being right, then surely the Gospel should have something to say about how a people who can have a shared past can go on by confessing their sin. Here it seems Christians have something constructive to offer to our politics. We have a story of sin and forgiveness forged in the practices of confession and reconciliation that at least offers the kind of hope Wolterstorff suggested we need. The claim that the first task of the church is to be the church, even in America, could turn out to be good news if the challenge before us as Americans is learning how to be a people who can make our past truthfully ours. That the church's first task is to be the church, therefore, is anything but a withdrawal strategy.

23. MacIntyre, "How to Be a North American," p. 18.
24. Some no doubt would assume that the war in Vietnam constitutes such a wrong, but I do not. The way the United States exited that war may well constitute such a wrong. Slavery and the genocide against the Native Americans are certainly places to begin to think about such wrongs.

Yet revival conversions have a well-deserved reputation for not lasting. As tempting as the strategy suggested in the last paragraph may be, I think it would be a mistake to try to make Christianity look good by supplying substance and practice that the liberal narratives of America cannot supply. The ascendancy of liberal ideology and practice in America could be seen as very good news for Christians. In fact, the very emptiness liberalism creates invites someone to fill the space. That Americans lack a strong moral account to justify and/or guide their relations to one another seems to make Christianity, or at least a surrogate, all the more necessary. Indeed, this can look like the best possible of all worlds, as Christianity gets to supply the morality without having to govern. Put in terms of the analysis above, Christianity becomes the master story to sustain a republic which officially can have no master story.

A story not unlike this has been tempting for liberal and conservative Christians alike. Liberal Christians assume something like a religious appeal is necessary or at least important to sustain the quest for justice; conservative Christians assume that without Christianity people cannot develop the virtues necessary to sustain a free society. Thus the importance of intermediate institutions of which the church seems to be a ready exemplification. Calls for Christians to make the family work are but the outworking of such strategies. The only problem is that the only institution more destructive of the family than capitalism is Christianity.

I am not entirely unsympathetic with some of the suggestions made by those who try to give Christians a role in American society shaped by these strategies. My problem is not that such strategies are wrong; rather, my problem is that this way of conceiving the relation of the church to American society makes the church less than the church. The problem, then, is not as I framed it in the title I first thought to give this paper—that is, "Why Christianity Will Never Work in America." Even though I believe that the fundamental presuppositions that shaped much of American life and government were meant to destroy or at least marginalize the church, I do believe that with God's help the church may even survive in America. Rather, the problem is that when Christians in America take as their fundamental task to make America work, then we lose our ability to survive as church. We do so because, in the interest of serving America, the church unwittingly becomes governed by the story of America that Marty tells. That is a story that is meant to make our God at home in America.

There is no better indication of the Americanization of the church than the god worshiped by Christians in America. For most American Christians, the crucially important thing about God is that God exist and that God's most important attribute be love. This is not a recent development but, if Thomas Jenkins is right, it began in the late eighteenth century in such figures as Timothy Dwight and was developed in the nineteenth century by such theologians as Noah Porter. In particular, Porter, drawing on the Enlightenment celebration of stoicism and modern science, emphasized the importance of emotional restraint and rationality. According to Jenkins,

> This centered on one trait in particular: benevolence. Benevolence was the key emotion emulated by people and ascribed to God. As the historian James Turner put it: "As the archetype of morality, God expressed the most elevated human ethics. He thus above all had to be—perhaps the favorite adjective of enlightenment divines—benevolent: disinterestedly willing the happiness of all his creatures."[25]

Jenkins traces the career of this god through the development of liberal and conservative theology and literary figures through the nineteenth and twentieth centuries. We should not be surprised that the result was a vague god vaguely worshiped or at least vaguely considered. For example, the influential liberal theologian, minister, and writer Theodore Munger drew on Thomas Arnold's understanding of

---

25. Thomas E. Jenkins, *The Character of God: Recovering the Lost Literary Power of American Protestantism* (New York: Oxford University Press, 1997), p. 21.

God as "a power not ourselves working for righteousness."[26] Such a view finds its most sophisticated expression in William James's suggestion that "God is the natural appellation, for us Christians at least, for the supreme reality, so I will call this higher part of the universe by the name of God."[27]

James's god, I believe, is not remarkably different from Reinhold Niebuhr's understanding of god. Of course Niebuhr's God was a god of judgment, but such judgment was, as Jenkins suggests, the expression of law, history, and the order of the world.[28] Christ was also the symbol of sacrificial love for Niebuhr, but the very language of symbol was used in order to protect against any need to make classical Christological claims that require Trinitarian displays of who God is. So, in spite of Niebuhr's reputation as one who attempted a recovery of orthodoxy, his account of God remained more theist than Christian—that is, a theism combined with a sentimental Christ. Niebuhr may well be the greatest representative of a theology shaped to make America work. But if that is the case, it is a deep judgment on the extent to which such theology has lost the reality of God found in cross and resurrection.

I am not suggesting that the American god Jenkins describes was the result of the Christian accommodation to America, but I do think that the attenuated god of American Christianity is necessary for a people who believe they are the future of humankind. I believe, therefore, that Christians can do nothing more significant in America than to be a people capable of worshiping a God who is to be found in the cross and resurrection of Jesus of Nazareth. The worship of such a God will not be good for any society that desires a god made in the image of the bureaucrat.[29] A people formed by the worship of a

---

26. Jenkins, *The Character of God,* pp. 137–38.

27. William James, *The Varieties of Religious Experience* (New York: Mentor Books, 1958), p. 425.

28. Jenkins, *The Character of God,* p. 169.

29. James (in his quite wonderfully obtuse restraint) observes when considering

crucified God, however, might just be complex enough to engage in the hard work of working out agreements and disagreements with others one small step at a time.

---

the character of what "over-beliefs" one might hold—"It would never do for us to place ourselves offhand at the position of a particular theology, the Christian theology, for example, and proceed immediately to define the 'more' as Jehovah, and the 'union' as his imputation to us of the righteousness of Christ. That would be unfair to other religions, and, for our present standpoint at least, would be an over-belief." *Varieties of Religious Understanding,* p. 431.

CONTRIBUTORS

Guy Bedouelle, O.P., holds doctoral degrees in law, history, and theology. He is rector of the Université Catholique de l'Ouest (Angers, France) and president of the Dominican Center of Studies (Paris). From 1999 until 2008, he was professor of church history at the University of Fribourg in Switzerland. He has authored many books on church history, spirituality, and art, including *Du spirituel dans le cinéma* (Cerf, Paris 1985/2006), *In the Image of St. Dominic* (Ignatius Press, San Francisco 1994), *History of the Church* (Continuum, London, New-York 2003), *La réforme du catholicisme* (Cerf, Paris 2002), *Une République, des religions* (Editions de l'Atelier, Paris 2003), *L'Église et la sexualité* (co-authored with Philippe Becquart and Jean-Louis Bruguès, Cerf, 2006).

Peter John Cameron, O.P., is the founding editor-in-chief of *Magnificat*. He is also a professor of homiletics, an award-winning playwright, and the artistic director of Blackfriars Repertory Theatre. He serves as the director of preaching for the Dominican Province of St. Joseph. Fr. Cameron has authored six books. The most recent is *Jesus, Present Before Me: Meditations for Eucharistic Adoration.*

John Haldane is professor of philosophy at the University of St. Andrews and director of its Centre for Ethics, Philosophy and Public Affairs. He is widely published in the areas of history of philosophy, metaphysics, philosophy of religion, philosophy of mind, and philosophy of value. He is the co-author (with J. J. C. Smart) of *Atheism and Theism,* 2d ed. (Blackwell, 2003), *An Intelligent Person's Guide to Religion* (Duckworth, 2003), *Faithful Reason* (Routledge, 2004), *The Church and the World*

(Gracewing, 2008), and *Seeking Meaning and Making Sense* (Imprint Academic, 2008). He also writes in the fields of art history and criticism, education and theology. In addition he is a frequent contributor to newspapers, radio, and television. His 2003–2004 Gifford Lectures were entitled *Mind, Soul and Deity.*

Stanley Hauerwas is Gilbert T. Rowe Professor of Theological Ethics at Duke Divinity School. He holds a Ph.D. from Yale and a D.D. from the University of Edinburgh. Professor Hauerwas has sought to recover the significance of the virtues for understanding the nature of the Christian life. He held the prestigious Gifford Lectureship at the University of St. Andrews, Scotland in 2001. His book *A Community of Character* was selected as one of the one hundred most important books on religion of the twentieth century. Among his numerous publications, he has recently authored *Matthew: Brazos Theological Commentary on the Bible* (Brazos, 2006), *The State of the University: Academic Knowledges and the Knowledge of God*, (Blackwell, 2007), and (with Romand Coles) *Christianity, Democracy, and the Radical Ordinary: Conversations between a Radical Democrat and a Christian* (Wipf and Stock, 2007).

Ralph McInerny, the Michael P. Grace Professor of Medieval Studies and professor of philosophy at Notre Dame, holds degrees from St. Paul Seminary, the University of Minnesota, and Laval University. He has taught at the University of Notre Dame since 1955 and was director of the Jacques Maritain Center from 1979 to 2006. He has served as president of the American Catholic Philosophical Association, The Metaphysical Society, and the Fellowship of Catholic Scholars. His Gifford Lectures, delivered in 1999–2000, were published under the title *Characters in Search of Their Author* (2001). Among his two dozen scholarly books are *Aquinas and Analogy, The Question of Christian Ethics,* and the Penguin Classic *Thomas Aquinas' Selected Writings.* He has also written more than eighty novels and is creator of the Father Dowling series of mysteries.

Daniel N. Robinson is distinguished professor, emeritus, at Georgetown University; a member of the philosophy faculty at Oxford University, and serves as visiting professor at the Institute for the Psychological Sciences. He holds awards for Lifetime Achievement and Distinguished Contributions from the American Psychological Association. His sixteen books, more than thirty edited and published volumes, and numerous articles and lectures, have addressed topics in the philosophy of science, intellectual history, philosophy of law, ethics, and the basic sciences. His most recent publication is *Consciousness and Mental Life* (Columbia University Press, 2008).

Craig Steven Titus is research professor at the Institute for the Psychological Sciences. He has written *Resilience and the Virtue of Fortitude: Aquinas in Dialogue with the Psychological Sciences* (2006), edited *The Person and the Polis: Faith and Values within the Secular State* (2006), *On Wings of Faith and Reason: The Christian Difference in Culture and Science* (2008), and coedited *The Pinckaers Reader: Renewing Thomistic Moral Theology* (2005) and *Sujet moral et communauté* (2007).

Carroll William Westfall is the Frank Montana Professor at the University of Notre Dame. He holds a Ph.D. from Columbia University. In his 1991 book, *Architectural Principles in the Age of Historicism* (Yale University Press), written with Robert Jan van Pelt, he studied the relationship between the history, theory, and practice of architecture. His study of Renaissance Rome was published as *In This Most Perfect Paradise* (1974). Professor Westfall's special interests are the history of the city and the American city; tradition and classicism in architecture; and the architect's capacity to nourish the Christian faith.

INDEX OF SUBJECTS

value/values, 1, 8–9, 126; American, 20, 142, 145; and art, 33, 43, 45; moral, 117. *See also* morality
vice, 90, 130, 143
virtue, 3; in America, 142; artistic, 6; intellectual, 3; and literature, 90, 92; moral, 4, 6; practical, 3; theological, 4, 132

war, 93; American Civil War, 78n17; Spanish Civil War, 93; Vietnam War, 147–48; World War I, 92; World War II, 5, 93
welfare 18, 125
well-being, moral, 12, 62, 66, 69
West, the, 2, 7, 9–10, 12–13, 20, 54, 60, 145. *See also* society, western
wisdom, 3, 18, 125, 132
wonder, 6n17, 7, 35
worship, 2, 4, 7, 19, 48, 58, 79, 129, 135, 143, 151

INDEX OF NAMES

The John Henry Cardinal Newman Lectures
EDITED BY CRAIG STEVEN TITUS

1. *The Person and the Polis: Faith and Values within the Secular State* (2007)

2. *On Wings of Faith and Reason: The Christian Difference in Culture and Science* (2008)

Monograph Series

Fergus Kerr, *"Work on Oneself": Wittgenstein's Philosophical Psychology* (2008)

Christianity and the West: Interaction and Impact in Art and Culture was designed and typeset in Minion by Kachergis Book Design of Pittsboro, North Carolina. It was printed on 55-pound Colonial White and bound by Lightning Source of La Vergne, Tennessee.

Printed in the United States
140064LV00002B/1/P